The Evolution of
RADIO...WITH PICTURES
WECT-TV's First Twenty Years
1954 – 1974

Compiled and Edited by Betty Hutson Perkins
With the invaluable assistance of
Wayne Jackson

Cover Design by Ronnie Hawes
Photo and Page Layout by C.L. Perkins

William Madison Randall Library,
University of North Carolina at Wilmington
Wilmington, NC

The Evolution of Radio…With Pictures
WECT-TV's First Twenty Years
1954 -1974

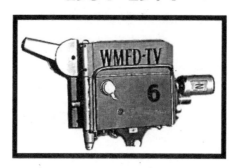

Copyright 2004 by Betty Hutson Perkins

Published in 2004 in the United States of America by William Madison Randall Library, University of North Carolina at Wilmington, 601 S. College Rd., Wilmington, NC 28403

The evolution of radio…with pictures : WECT-TV's first twenty years 1954-1974 / compiled and edited by Betty Hutson Perkins with the invaluable assistance of Wayne Jackson. ; cover design by Ronnie Hawes.

p. cm.

ISBN 0-9749993-0-X

1. WECT-TV (Television Station, Wilmington, N.C.)—History. 2. Television stations—North Carolina—Wilmington—History. 3. Television broadcasting—North Carolina—Wilmington—History. I. Perkins, Betty Hutson.

HE8700.8 E96 2004

ACKNOWLEDGEMENTS

First, I want to express my heartfelt thanks to the University of North Carolina at Wilmington and to Mr.Dan Cameron for their generosity in funding the publication of this book.

My thanks also go to Mr. Sherman Hayes, University Librarian at UNCW, for pointing me in the right direction by recognizing it as a "historic resource" for today's students of television and communications.

And, my grateful appreciation to all of those employees of WECT during those exciting first twenty years who took the time to sort out their memories of those days and put them down on paper. Equally, to those who shared their prized photographs in order to help bring those memories to life.

To my husband, C.L. Perkins (former WECT chief photographer) without whose computer expertise this book would probably be lost somewhere in cyber-space.

And especially to Wayne Jackson, my former boss, a fountain of information and collector of an amazing amount of documentation about those great first twenty years.

For me, putting this book together was a labor of love, a way of reliving a time in my career that had an enormous impact on my life.

Betty Hutson Perkins
March, 2004

1954

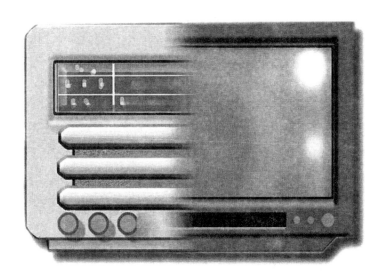

1974

Table of Contents
Listed by author

Time Line

April 9, 1954   Our first day! 5 hours, 12 commercials.

Sept. 27, 1954   Schedule expanded to include daytime programming.

Oct. 15, 1954   Hurricane Hazel. Channel 6 gives viewers first comprehensive coverage of a local disaster.

Feb. 18, 1955   We're interconnected. Live network programs.

April, 1955   Our first remote telecast, The Azalea Festival Parade. One camera, long cable from studio to street.

Oct. 1, 1956   We go mornings, too, with live network programming.

June 1, 1957   We're a regional giant now. Full power, tall tower, 18 hours a day.

Oct. 1957   Ownership changes. The Atlantic Telecasting Corporation replaces WMFD-TV, Inc.

Dec. 1957   We are colorful too, with network color shows.

Feb. 15, 1958   Something new is added, new call letters - WECT-TV.

Sept. 7, 1958   "Take off" for the first of four big air shows. Becomes the biggest in the nation, with over 100,000 attendance.

Sept. 1958   Station owned micro-wave relay goes into operation.

April, 1959   It's moving day. New building, new look.

April 19, 1960   We start a new trend in politics, the television rally, for gubernatorial candidate Dr. I. Beverly Lake.

Oct. 1960   We break precedent, telecast live for the first time an all-day public hearing before the Highway Commission at Thalian Hall.

Oct. 1961   The Battleship U.S.S. North Carolina arrives in Wilmington harbor. A dream originated by WECT-TV account executive Jimmy Craig. We lead fund raising with statewide telecast and broadcast arrival and later dedication.

Summer, 1962   We're building again. New addition to house two RCA video tape units. New era in local production.

April, 1963   Another first. We televise live the General Assembly session aboard the Battleship. First legislative telecast outside of Raleigh.

May, 1967   Building expansion again. New lobby, 10 offices, another studio and more storage space.

March, 1968   Local programs go color as we put two color studio cameras in operation. WECT-TV is a full-color station now.

March 12, 1969   2,000 feet tall! The new giant tower and transmitter near White Lake doubles our coverage area, and we reach hundreds of thousands of new viewers.

June, 1972   WECT-TV goes public with stock. Thousands of shares sold in just a few days.

Sept. 5, 1973   First labor vote. Employees support management and vote down bid by CWA for union representation.

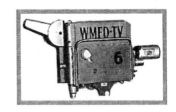

How This Book Happened... and Why
Betty (Hutson) Perkins

Several years ago a group of us...all "alumni" of the first twenty years of southeastern North Carolina's first television station, originally known as WMFD-TV...got together to meet old friends, compare memories and brag about subsequent accomplishments. This first gathering led to sort-of-annual get togethers and, of course, much conversation about the "good old days".

It occurred to us that today's TV watchers are so accustomed to all its bells and whistles, the magical special effects and images direct from outer space that they probably can't imaging how low-tech our hi-tech was when local television made its first five hours- a- day foray into the living rooms of Wilmington and vicinity.

That was in 1954, a half century in time and light years ago in technology.

WMFD's (which later became the present WECT-TV) first studio was in a downtown Wilmington building in a creaky third floor area. There was one camera, two lights, a couple of mikes, a bare-bones control room, and ONLY ONE PERSON who had ever worked in television before.

And since no one there knew enough about this relatively recent invention to know that they couldn't possibly make it work with what they had, it worked...albeit with a glitch or two here and there!

I am told that early on, one very frustrated engineer beset with technical woes was heard to remark that "God never meant for pictures to fly through the air!" Obviously, time has proved him wrong.

In those first years, everything was done "live", so a mistake was a mistake...a goof was a goof, there for everybody who owned one of the prized television sets to see (and sometimes to remember and talk about for years to come.)

According to "reliable sources" Mr. Dick Dunlea Sr., the station's original owner, sometimes referred to television as "Picture Radio"...hence the name of this book.

I note that a phrase has recently been coined that exactly fits almost everyone's job description in those years..."multi-tasking". We just called it "doing whatever you need to do to get the program on the air".

Today, when we take for granted remote telecasts with video and sound simultaneously originating from the four corners of the world, the first staffers remember when the "remoteness" of the first remote telecast was governed by how far the cable could reach on the sidewalk outside the studio.

So here, in order that today's viewers can read about and remember how it all started in this particular corner of our state, we offer, in their own words, the reminiscences of some of the many people who passed through the studio doors of WMFD-WECT-TV during those first twenty years.

The giant antenna for WMFD-TV's transmitter, located on the banks of the Cape Fear River near Orton Road, is tuned by technicians before being raised. Regular programs from Wilmington's first television station began on April 9, 1954. The antenna weighed two and a half tons.

A Page From The Past
Dan Cameron

Back in the mid-thirties, Mr. R.A. Dunlea, Sr., put radio station WRAM on the air in Wilmington, operating out of the old Wilmington Hotel in very meager quarters. This was the city's first radio station, and a very successful business from the start.

I don't know why my father got interested in the radio business, but he invested with Mr. Dunlea and owned forty percent of the business (now WMFD)

In the early fifties the F.C.C. allocated Channel 6 to this area and Mr. Dunlea applied for and got permission to build a TV station here. He formed a company and again my family took forty percent ownership.

Dan D. Cameron

R.A. "Dick" Dunlea Jr., fresh out of college, was the first president, Mr. Dunlea Sr. was Chairman of the Board, and Mrs. Dunlea, my brother Bruce and I served on the Board of Directors.

The original studio was located on the third floor of a building just off Third Street on Princess, on the floor above the radio station. This turned out to be rather convenient, since at first many members of the staff served double duty. What wasn't so convenient was the fact that there was no elevator, so it was tough on advertisers to get their merchandise up those narrow stairs and in front of the camera.

Dick Dunlea Sr.

Initially, business was hard to come by because there were so few television sets in this market area, and merchants were skeptical about this relatively new media.

The Dunleas did a great job of attracting first class radio people to the new station, although few if any of those first staffers had any television experience. Some of the early programming had a mark of genius, since there was only one camera, no tape machines, no remote facilities, and limited space.

Using hard work, ingenuity, and an ability to invent things as they went along, that staff did a super job.

In 1957, the Dunleas decided they wanted to get out of the TV business so I put a group together to buy out their interest. I was elected President of the corporation, and held that position for the next 35 years.

I can't think of a better way to have spent my life.

WMFD-TV
CHANNEL 6
WILMINGTON,N.C.

We Were All Radio People
By Bob West

Bob West

When Channel Six signed on the air April 9, 1954 we were all radio people. John McNeill had worked for a few months in the photo lab at WFMY-TV in Greensboro. Nobody else had any TV experience at all. From top management all the way down, the staff of WMFD-TV consisted almost entirely of radio people. No TV types in 1954. Because we were radio people, when it came to television we didn't know what we could do. More importantly, we didn't know what we couldn't do.

Dick Dunlea, Sr. started putting radio stations on the air in the 1920's. He signed on WMFD in April of 1935. His background was as a Coast Guard wireless radio operator. We affectionately called him The Captain. Radio, maritime or broadcast, was his first love. He turned the management of the TV station over to his son, Dick, Jr. The Captain called Channel Six "picture radio." We did seem to be more radio than TV. Our television studio, control room, art department and prop room were on the top floor of a three story building on Princess Street near the corner with Third Street. A piano company/record store was on the first floor, the radio station on the second and all the office staff, salesmen, engineering, everything else was combined with radio.

Nobody would put a TV studio on a third floor, with no elevator. WMFD-TV did. The third floor had been a dance hall of some type during World War 11. For television it was divided into a medium sized studio, a film room, a control room and space for the film and slide projectors. In 1954 all commercials were either live camera, film or slides. When MacMillan and Cameron wanted to advertise a washing machine, a dryer, a refrigerator and a chest type freezer, their delivery people had to negotiate three flights of very steep stairs and our production folks had to lug the heavy appliances into and out of the studio on very short notice.

The Way It Was . . . April, 1954

Bob Caudle, Clint Long, Charlie Castleberry in Control Room

WMFD-TV's First Studio

Furniture store delivery folks complained when they had to carry up heavy sofa beds, bedroom suites, china cabinets and dining room tables to the third floor. A deliveryman for Carolina Furniture once told me he really wished they would just advertise table lamps. Although it was a backbreaking struggle up the stairs, most delivery folks were good-natured about it. Everybody wanted to see what a TV station looked like. I was about to say a real TV station but, I'm not sure we were really representative of the nation's TV stations those first few months. I do know we were happy to help carry up any thing any merchant wanted to advertise.

Advertisers were hard to find those first few weeks. But it took only about a month for the sale of TV sets to catch on and people to realize that television would have a real impact on Wilmington and southeastern North Carolina.

I came to WMFD two days after the TV station signed on. I had just turned 21, born and raised in Wilmington. We had moved away after the seventh grade. I was working at WRRF Radio in Washington, North Carolina and I had seen Channel 9 in Greenville sign on the year before and what an impact it had had on the radio stations. After a month or two it seemed nobody cared about radio anymore. I could see it was time to branch out. I applied to all of the half dozen TV stations in North Carolina. Wilmington wasn't on the air when I applied, but they were looking for an announcer to cover the night radio shift when the rest of the staff was working on the TV side. I came down in March and looked it over and I figured if I got on the radio staff, I could find a way to get to television. I gave notice in little Washington and joined WMFD during the first week it was on the air.

The station had no live network affiliation. We carried a half dozen half- hour film programs, including the once-a-week Life Of Riley from NBC, sponsored by the Gulf Oil Company. The Wilmington oil distributor had put pressure on the Gulf ad agency to place the program on Channel Six. We had two or three syndicated programs, including Where The Heart Is and Victory At Sea. They had bought a package of very old wrestling programs, an even older collection of westerns, and a sorry assortment of the few grade B movies that were available for television in 1954. Everything else was entirely local.

The station signed on at six o'clock in the early evening with "Over At Al's." Al Compton was the WMFD Radio morning announcer. He was a warm, friendly personality that everybody liked. "Over At Al's" was the most ambitious of the local programs. A hillbilly band from just across the state line in South Carolina had been hired to provide the music. For television they were the Rhythm Range Riders, complete with western clothes and cowboy boots. The Riders were Bob Hickman,

C.O. "Hayseed" Thomas, Tex Lancaster, Bob Hickman, Freddie Hickman

his brother Freddie and "Tex" Lancaster. The girl vocalist was "Twiddle" Perry. C.O. Thomas played a country bumpkin comedian named "Hayseed. A set had been built that was supposed to look like the front porch of a log cabin. The entire set was only about 20 feet long, rough looking but that fit a rustic log cabin setting just fine. Remember most of the set builders were all radio people. Al and company became an instant hit.

There was no other TV signal available in Wilmington. The people on the air became celebrities over night. The Wilmington folks soon were treating this group of radio announcers as if they were movie stars. It was a giddy time.

Clint Long, a native of Morehead City and a war veteran who had worked in North Carolina radio for several years, had assembled most of the TV staff. His title was Program Director, but he handled most of the on-the-air operations. Clint did the weather report, Clay McBride news, Bob Caudle sports, and Johnny Thomas was both an on-the-air cowboy host for Western Theatre and also the staff musician. Johnny could play jazz piano with the best of them, and still does. Johnny was the youngest of the group, just 19, all the others were in their early or mid twenties.

The news, sports and weather programs began at 6:30 PM right after "Over At Al's" and the news set was right next to the log cabin. In fact every set was right next to another one or was pulled away and replaced with something else. By way of sets, we are talking about a couple of sheets of plywood nailed to the wall or mounted on a small rolling dolly. I think Clint had seen sets like this in a TV book he bought. He and a few others had visited other TV stations before sign-on, but there was no real TV experience. We were all radio people.

Clay McBride was also a war veteran with radio experience. He read the news. His "set" was a sheet of Masonite painted white with a crude globe drawn on it. Clay read mostly wire copy from the radio station United Press machine. He used an occasional still picture or two. These were glued to 12 by 14 cardboards and propped up on the desk. If he wanted to show a picture, the program had to be arranged so the director could throw up a slide with "Today's News Pictures" before the camera could move in for a close-up of the photographs. It is in this type of production that Channel Six in Wilmington was different from any other station in North Carolina and as far as we know, different from any other station in the country. WMFD-TV had only one studio camera.

"You can't do TV with just one camera!" That's what the RCA sales engineer had told Dick Dunlea Senior and Junior, until the salesman realized that he was only going to sell one camera, no matter what. "Well, I guess you could do it with one. I've just never heard of it." Neither had anyone else, but we did it.

Clint and his group of radio people managed to work around this monumental problem. There was no zoom lens. To get from a wide lens to a medium to a close-up you had to turn by hand the turret that carried the three lenses. This looked really bad on the air. So to get from one lens to another you had to go to a slide first. Film and slides were on the same film chain and the only other source of on-the-air picture was that one lone bulky RCA studio camera on a budget priced tripod with three medium sized wheels. Most often the best way to get from wide shot to close-up was to physically roll the camera across the uneven wooden floor that had been worn out by thousands of dancers over the years.

Harold Ludwig, a Wilmington still photographer, was hired to make all the pictures and the slides and also operate the live studio camera. Harold became a master at rolling that balky monster over the rough terrain of the floor. The staff rehearsed for about two weeks before signing on and the people who were there for the rehearsals said Captain Dunlea at one point was almost ready to admit it was going to be hard to do programs with just the one camera.

But hard or not we were going to do it. As the rehearsals went on, Harold became better and better at navigating that floor without the viewers getting seasick. He became a master at this skill that was not required in any other TV station anywhere. Harold could go from a wide shot of seven refrigerators to a close-up of the butter keeper of one of them just as smoothly as you could have wanted and in the matter of a second or two.

He was a master. John McNeill, who had the only real TV experience, got very good at it, but since John had worked in a TV station with more than one camera, he did know you couldn't move a camera like that. John learned to do it very well, but Harold Ludwig remained the champion one camera operator of all time. Worldwide, as far as I know.

The floor was so bad that it was not only rough when the camera rolled over it, it also squeaked so loudly it would drown out what someone was saying. Clint had an idea. He called it a "work party." Clint was a natural born leader. Everybody brought a hammer from home and for about an hour before we signed on, we all got down on our hands and knees and pounded nails into that floor. Announcers, engineers, everybody. Everybody except the Rhythm Range Riders. Some how they were excused but the rest of us raised such a howl that they were soon included in Clint's "party." It helped the floor a little bit.

After Clay read the news, Clint presented the weather. He had chosen weather for himself because it took the most preparation and I suspect because it would look the most like a real TV program. He had a national and a local map painted on a series of black boards that were green. He drew in the fronts and the highs and lows with chalk. He got all of his information every day with a very long hour and a half telephone

Clint Long and his Hi-Tech Weather Maps

conversation with the Wilmington weather bureau. Between the various camera shots, slides announcing "Today's Temperatures" and "Tomorrow's Forecast" allowed the camera to move from one set of maps or charts to another. Clint took his role as a TV Weather Reporter very seriously and despite the low tech appearance of the program I believe he presented as complete a TV weather report as has ever been done, anywhere at anytime.

Bob Caudle, another North Carolina native and radio veteran, followed the weather with a sports report. Again mostly reading wire copy and once in a while, a local photograph that Harold Ludwig or John McNeill had taken with the Speed Graphic camera the radio station used for publicity pictures. This is the very large and awkward camera you see associated with newspaper photographers of the 30's and 40's. The sheets of film were fitted into metal holders and these were inserted into the camera for each shot. It was real easy to forget to move all the film holders correctly. In other words, it was not what a TV station needed to cover the news. It's what we had and we didn't know you weren't supposed to cover the news and sports this way. We were all radio people. We didn't know you couldn't do it this way.

Besides the sports, Bob Caudle did another program that quickly caught on with the audience. It started out as a video disc jockey program titled "TV Song Shop." There were no music videos but Bob played phonograph records and we showed the turntable going around and around and occasionally a three-minute film clip of some very bad Latin American musicians that we had bought from some fast-talking film salesman.

Very shortly after Bob began this series, Stan Rehder of the Wilmington florist Rehders, showed up at the station with an idea. He could do a number of voices and was adept at operating a hand puppet. Hester was born. Stan modified an existing hand puppet disguising its true identity to satisfy copyright laws. I don't know why we were so careful there, we sure weren't that careful anywhere else. But more on that later. Stan played Hester as a wisecracking foil to Bob's smooth straight man. Hester was Charlie McCarthy to Bob's Edgar Bergen. "Bob and Hester" was an instant hit. The set was modified to look sort of like Kukla, Fran and Ollie.

Bob Caudle and the irrepressible "Hester", aka Stan Rehder (under the desk)

The topic of conservation on the streets of Wilmington the next morning was what Hester had said to Bob the night before. We soon found out what a popular force television was going to be. Nobody was talking about Amos 'n Andy or Edgar and Charlie anymore. They were talking about Bob Caudle and Hester.

The early popularity of local television, the new kid on the entertainment block, was never underlined any better than by what happened at a Wilmington movie theater soon after the station signed on. Johnny Thomas, a recent New Hanover High School graduate and the youngest of the radio people, put on a cowboy costume and became "Johnny Ranger" every night. His background was also radio. He was the night shift announcer at WMFD radio that I was replacing. He had even done a student radio program while still in high school. He was a TV star now.

Johnny stood in front of a rear-screen projector that had a old west landscape and he introduced some very old grade "C" western movies. One of the downtown movie theater operators thought it would be a good idea to have Johnny Ranger live on the theater stage one Saturday morning as part of a kid's doubleheader of western movies. Of course Johnny talked it up on the air.

"All you Junior Rangers meet me at the movies this Saturday morning, don't forget." Johnny reminded them every day for a week and they didn't forget. Two hours before the live appearance of Johnny Ranger, there was a line around two city blocks waiting to see the TV star. And by the way, it was raining.

There was no doubt, these radio people were stumbling themselves into the living rooms and the hearts of residents of this historic port city. Much of the credit goes not only to the announcers themselves but also to Clint Long. He had to have the knack of a talent scout to assemble such a strong group. The original Channel Six announcing staff of Clint, Bob, Clay, Al and Johnny was the strongest group of local on-the-air-TV announcers I have ever seen. Remember this was 50 years ago and we were all radio people. We didn't know you couldn't entertain a whole region with all local programs. We didn't know, so we did it.

I was the first announcer added to the original five. While working the night radio shift, I spent a lot of my own time during the day learning what I needed to know about TV. After about two weeks, Clint agreed to let me audition to see how I would do on camera. One afternoon, before we signed on, he gave me four or five news stories from the wire machine and gave me a half hour or so to read them over before going on camera. I had prepared for an opportunity. For several months I had been practicing memorizing about five minutes of news. I would do it at night in my rented room in little Washington waiting for my chance. There were no teleprompters. Everybody else read the copy from the desk, looking up as much as possible.

When I auditioned I didn't look down at all. In a half hour I had managed to commit to memory the 90 seconds or so of wire copy. Clint was duly impressed, although he didn't let me know how pleased he was. I found out later. I was told I could do News Capsule at 9 o'clock at night, if I could get somebody to cover for me on the radio station for about 15 minutes around nine. Bob and Clay agreed to help me out. News Capsule came on after Johnny's westerns and a film show or two and just before - believe it or not - The Late Show.

Yes, on WMFD-TV in Wilmington, North Carolina in the spring of 1954, The Late Show came on at 9:05PM.

The station had bought that package of bad old movies and that's what we programmed as the Late Show. Our Late Show ended pretty early, at about 11 o'clock.

I took my five minutes of TV news very seriously. My radio shift was very busy until about 7 o'clock and then we joined the ABC Radio network for two hours. I would pick out the news stories I was going to use for television before joining the network. Then for two hours I would walk back and forth in the long hallway on the second floor that served as the news ticker room, rehearsing the copy so completely that I had it memorized by 8:30. That first Monday night when I did News Capsule for the first time, I was nervous, but I was so confident that I had it memorized that I didn't look down a single time. I had practiced a distinctive sign off for the program - that was the custom in those days. When I finished the news I looked down at my wristwatch and said, "Now there's only time left to say Goodnight." Sure it was corny, but it worked and the first addition to the original five announcer staff was Bob West.

It didn't take very long for TV news to catch on in Wilmington. A reporter for the Star-News newspapers had gotten a tip from the Wilmington Police Department that they were investigating a pornography case involving photographs taken by a male instructor at Wilmington College. The police were ready to break the case and the reporter was ready to break his story when the ownership at the newspaper killed the story. The reporter was so outraged he resigned, but he also came to me and told me about the story. He offered to fill me in on all the details, so I could be ready to go on the air with the story the moment the police started making arrests.

I brought Clint in and he said to go ahead and work with the reporter and the police getting the background and we would broadcast the story as soon as the police gave the go-ahead. I was getting the background when Captain Dunlea got a call from the president of one of the station's most important advertisers. It seems a member of his family was somehow involved. He demanded that the station kill the story or he would cancel all of his advertising with both the TV and the radio station.

Captain Dunlea called Clint and me into his office and asked us if we believed the story to be true. I told him the police were going to make a series of charges within a day or two, and they felt they had a very strong case. "When the police file the charges, you break the story. And don't worry about the sponsor, I'll call him right now and tell him we will run the story." Then the Captain winked and said, "In fact I'll really enjoy telling him he can't intimidate us."

When the police made the arrests, we ran the story and it was an exclusive, the very first for TV in Wilmington. We had no movie camera and couldn't shoot stills of the arrests, so we ran the story as all desk copy, but we had all the facts and the extensive background provided by the former newspaper reporter. Now he and I both knew why the paper had killed his story. It gave all of us such a feeling of pride that the ownership of our station had backed us up and stood firmly against an important advertiser.

The Captain had more or less told him to go jump into Greenfield Lake. I believe the advertiser did actually cancel for a short time, but his competitors were using TV advertising so he had to come back whether he really wanted to or not.

The impact of TV advertising was probably the most astounding aspect of our all local TV station. One of the most amazing success stories involved a small open-air grocery market on Greenfield Street. Nick's Market started running a commercial within the first few weeks and Nick insisted that he do his own talking and talk he did. We never really did know how much time Nick bought, but the commercials seemed to run about 15 minutes. And we never knew what he was going to say. Nick brought about half his store up to our third floor. He piled vegetables and meats on a table, stood behind them and in his thickly accented English entertained us all.

"You can't beat Nick's meat." That was one of his favorites. Another was, "Nick has the lowest nuts in town and they won't be any higher next week." Did he know what he was saying? You bet he did. Without really trying, Nick Saleeby found a way to use this new advertising tool and he sold merchandise. What had been a marginal market in a less traveled part of town suddenly became the most talked about grocery store in Wilmington.

WMFD-TV — SOUTHEASTERN NORTH CAROLINA - - NORTHEASTERN

FILM TIME ONLY

CLASS "A" RATES

6:00 PM-11:00 PM—Monday through Friday
4:00 PM-11:00 PM—Saturday and Sunday

	1 ti.	26 tis.	52 tis.	104 tis.	156 tis.	260 tis.
1 Hour	$200.00	$190.00	$180.00	$170.00	$160.00	$150.00
45 Minutes	160.00	152.00	144.00	136.00	128.00	120.00
40 Minutes	150.00	142.50	135.00	127.50	120.00	112.50
30 Minutes	120.00	114.00	108.00	102.00	96.00	90.00
20 Minutes	100.00	95.00	90.00	85.00	80.00	75.00
15 Minutes	80.00	76.00	72.00	68.00	64.00	60.00
10 Minutes	70.00	66.50	63.00	59.50	56.00	52.50
5 Minutes	50.00	47.50	45.00	42.50	40.00	37.50
1 Min. 20 Seconds	34.00	32.30	30.60	28.90	27.20	25.50
10 Seconds	19.00	18.15	17.30	16.45	15.60	14.75

10 SEC -

FILM TIME ONLY

CLASS "B" RATES

All other times than shown in Class "A"

	1 ti.	26 tis.	52 tis.	104 tis.	156 tis.	260 tis.
1 Hour	$150.00	$142.50	$135.00	$127.50	$120.00	$112.50
45 Minutes	120.00	114.00	108.00	102.00	96.00	90.00
40 Minutes	112.00	106.40	100.80	95.20	89.60	84.00
30 Minutes	90.00	85.50	81.00	76.50	72.00	67.50
20 Minutes	75.00	71.25	67.50	63.75	60.00	56.25
15 Minutes	60.00	57.00	54.00	51.00	48.00	45.00
10 Minutes	52.00	49.40	46.80	44.20	41.60	39.00
5 Minutes	37.00	35.15	33.30	31.45	29.60	27.75
1 Min. to 20 Seconds	26.00	24.70	23.40	22.10	20.80	19.50
10 Seconds	17.00	16.15	15.30	14.45	13.60	12.75

10 Second Station breaks in both "A" & "B" time must share Audio station identification.

LIVE RATES QUOTED ON REQUEST

This rate card is published for the convenient reference of advertisers and agencies and is not to be considered as an offer of facilities. The rates are subject to change without notice.

Nick was just one of the success stories. Most advertisers preferred that one of our announcers do their spots. There was no tape and no local film. All commercials were live and most of them involved lots of merchandise brought up those steep flights of steps. Commercials were sold as 60-second spots, but most of them ran longer, some much longer. The station management was so intent on proving that television could sell goods and services that they didn't really put a strict time limit on the spots.

As you can imagine, that caused chaos as far as program timing was concerned. Many, many months later a memo came out from sales manager Claud O'Shields. "Starting immediately no 60 second commercial will run longer than two and a half minutes."

While all this seems so bizarre today, in 1954 WMFD-TV was not only brand new, it was also under-funded and in a very small TV market. No one had seen television of any kind before we signed on. If the station was going to be a success it was going to have to be popular not only with the viewers but also with the advertisers.

The Star-News newspapers had ignored the advent of television in Wilmington. There was no mention of any kind about the station in the news columns when we signed on. The only way anyone reading the paper in April 1954 would have known anything about television was in a MacMillan and Cameron half page ad advertising TV sets.

When I came to town to interview for the job in March there were no TV sets in the hotels or anywhere else. That changed very quickly. With very little equipment, a very tight budget and a bunch of radio people, we sort of made up television as we went along and it worked. Did it ever work? It worked so well, the station expanded the staff.

Two more announcers were added that summer. Don Foreman and Wayne Jackson came from the same radio station in Rocky Mount. Don was an all-purpose staff announcer and Wayne was hired to do an hour and a half program from 4:30 PM to six o'clock in the afternoon every day. Yes, we were increasing our airtime by a big chunk. The program was "Relax With Jax" and it broke new ground in the saga of radio people figuring out television as we went along. I was the co-producer and director for the program and we had to figure out how to fill 90 minutes of airtime everyday. Wayne brought in a lot of guests from the community and interviewed every visiting celebrity that came to town.

We filled some of the time by playing phonograph records, but we had to have something to show on the screen while the records were playing. Wayne came up with a lot of ideas. One of my favorites was Turtle Races. We went to the pet department at Woolworth's Five and Dime on Front Street and bought six or seven of the little two inch box turtles that children kept as pets in a little plastic dish with a green plastic palm tree. We painted numbers on the back of our turtles and marked out a track with seven lanes on a tabletop. While a record of Frankie Laine's "Mule Train" or some other popular song provided the audio, our one camera focused on the turtles. Some times one or two of the turtles would move, but very slowly. That was the point. Turtle races take a long time and time is what "Relax With Jax" had plenty of.

We decided to have a Halloween Party. It was a simple idea. We would have bobbing for apples, pin the tail on the donkey and other children's games. We invited the kids to come in costume and to bring their parents. We asked them to be at the station about an hour before airtime. When Wayne and I arrived an hour before that to get ready for the program there was already a line up the steps and down to Princess Street and around the corner. We estimated then that there were already more people in line than could ever fit in the studio. When we opened the third floor the crowd rushed into and completely filled the studio. The one camera was located in the center of the studio and the kids and their parents pushed toward it. When we went on the air I could not see the camera or Wayne or anything else through the control room window, except hundreds of children and their parents.

Trying to do the planned program was impossible. Parents would pick up their children and hold them in front of the camera lens, almost always too close to be in focus. It was chaos. We had planned prizes for the Best Costumes, the Cutest Girl, the Most Handsome Boy but it was almost impossible to do anything. Two or three times Wayne made his way to a corner of the studio where he was supposed to do a commercial, but the camera had trouble finding him.

Finally, after almost an hour and a half, we decided we had to clear the studio because other programs and more commercials were scheduled. We cut "Relax With Jax" short and ran an episode of the 15-minute free film, "Industry on Parade." The National Association of Manufacturers supplied the film free and it was our standby when we needed something to run in a hurry.

The program featured the manufacturing process of various products. You might see 15 minutes on how a wood products plant made both fence posts and toothpicks or the assembly line for sewing machines. This filler film became so popular we made it part of the regular schedule at one time.

This day it gave us time to politely ask our visitors to leave. Hardly anybody was happy. " I didn't get a chance for Suzy to be on television," one angry mother howled as we led them down the steps to the street. It was an experiment in live local TV that certainly proved the popularity of the medium but cost us some good will when we got a lot more than we had bargained for.

The biggest news story of 1954 changed the way people thought of television and Channel Six. Hurricane Hazel came up the mouth of the Cape Fear River on October 15th. We had begun to prepare for what the radio and TV stations would do the day before. An announcer and a cameraman would be sent to Carolina Beach and another two-man team would go to Wrightsville Beach.

John McNeill and I got the Wrightsville assignment. We only had the one Speed Graphic still camera, but Dick Dunlea, Junior had a personal 16 mm Kodak home movie camera. John McNeill

Hurricane Hazel, striking just months after we went on the air, presented a tremendous challenge to our inexperienced and ill- equipped news staff.

took it and his own still camera and we went to Station One. As the storm struck, all of us were supplying news for both WMFD Radio and TV. Television lost power in the middle of the worst hurricane of the century and we relied entirely on radio, which stayed on the air longer.

The TV audience with battery powered radios switched to 630 on the AM dial. It was almost like we continued to do television audio on the radio. John and I spent the first few hours of the storm on Wrightsville Beach and John shot movie film of the high winds and tides and houses and cottages being blown away. He got a series of shots of me up to my waist in a flooded telephone booth at Station One while calling in a report to the station. Chief Everett Williamson of the Wrightsville Beach Police Department tried to evacuate most of the residents.

Finally at the height of Hazel's fury he moved his officers, public works folks and John and me to the higher ground of Babies Hospital on the mainland. After the eye passed, the only vehicle that had any chance of making it back across the causeway to the oceanfront was a town dump truck. John and I caught a ride and he got some of the very first pictures of the devastation of the very severe hurricane. It was the 16th before John and I got back to the station. He had the very first movie film of this national disaster, but there was one big catch. Kodak put a black backing on this 16mm film, so it could only be developed back at the Kodak factory. Harold Ludwig believed that there must be some way to develop it in his darkroom. Clint decided it was worth a try.

Harold used a small hand cranked developing machine, but he couldn't get the backing off until a strip of film touched some Duz washing powder that was on the edge of his sink. The black backing came off. Harold took the bold step of dumping Duz and water into an empty ten-gallon crockery planter that was stored in the men's rest room. The backing came off.

"Duz does everything." Harold shouted as he mimicked the washing powder's familiar slogan.

Duz took the backing off, but it also took part of the film's emulsion off, so that footage of Hurricane Hazel looks pretty primitive. It should. It was shot with a home movie camera, processed in a crock-pot and dried by putting up several clotheslines in the studio and hanging the film across them. Every place where the film touched the clothesline more of the image came off. That film, which is still an important part of the historic documentation of Hurricane Hazel, was another example of a group of people who didn't know enough about television or film to know that you couldn't do this or you couldn't do that. We didn't know, so we did it.

If Channel Six hadn't been a big part of Wilmington life before Hazel, it certainly was after. We helped coordinate rescue and relief; we helped find housing and transportation for those that were left homeless. We became the official outlet for City, County and State agencies needing to communicate with the public. I remember so well Governor Luther Hodges coming to the command post at Babies Hospital soon after the storm to show the flag and reassure everyone that the state would do all it could to clean up the mess and help in the rebuilding.

A few days after the storm, John McNeill and I flew with pilot Jack Bennett of the Pennington Flying Service to survey the damage on the Brunswick County beaches. Jack flew the Star-News newspapers to Myrtle Beach every afternoon so he knew the landscape of that part of the coast very well. Jack got disoriented because not only the cottages were gone, but also the land. Hazel and Channel Six will always be thought of together when 1954 is reviewed.

A graphic example of how a bunch of radio people lucked into television, with what was probably divine guidance, happened a few weeks after the storm. Since we had the only film of both the storm and its aftermath, one of the national insurance companies wanted our footage and was willing to pay for it. They wanted the film put together with narration and music. I volunteered, but it was hard to find time in the control room and announce booth to do it. One afternoon, before we signed on, I got the film racked up and went in the announce booth to read the script I had written.

We signed on in 35 minutes so I only had this half hour to do this 30-minute program. I had a classical recording of Debussy's La Mer (The Sea) cued up. I started the music when the film came up. The first few minutes were scenes John had shot at Wrightsville Beach with high winds and heavy rain and cottages being heavily damaged. The music was fast paced and fit the images exactly. Then to my dismay I realized I had the 33 and 1/3 LP running at the 45-rpm speed. I reached over and changed speeds at the exact moment the film scenes changed from the raging storm to the devastation of the aftermath. It worked perfectly. The insurance company showed the completed program all over the country. If we had hired a live orchestra and a team of technicians the music and pictures couldn't have matched better. It was blind luck and we had a lot of that in 1954.

By the next hurricane season we were better prepared. We had learned a lot of lessons from Hazel. By the time Connie and Diane blew through one right after the other in a one-week period in August of 1955 we had announcers and photographers already assigned. John McNeill and I drew Wrightsville Beach again. Both storms, one on August 12'h and the other on the 17t", did hundreds of thousands of dollars in damage and caused widespread flooding.

A month later, on September 17th, Hurricane Ione slammed into the coast and gave Southeastern North Carolina its fourth major hurricane in less than a year. In 1955 we had a Bolex movie camera, a way to process the film, and a little better grasp on just what a TV station could do in a time of natural disaster.

WMFD-TV was the nerve center of hurricane preparedness, storm coverage and rescue and recovery. Channel Six really was "Your Hurricane Information Center." Even in 1955, we still didn't know a little local station with inadequate equipment and little television experience could cover major news stories better than the other stations in North and South Carolina, because the stories were happening in our front yard.

We had proved that earlier in 1955. The major spring festival in the Carolinas was the Wilmington Azalea Festival in early April and the main feature of the Festival was an elaborate parade through downtown Wilmington on Saturday morning. We thought we could telecast the parade live. We didn't know better.

Remember now we had no remote equipment of any kind. All we had was that one bulky, balky RCA studio camera. Clint figured a way to do the parade and nobody could talk him out of it. Our studio was around the corner from Third and Princess Streets. The parade-reviewing stand was on the City Hall steps at Third and Princess. We arranged for the camera to be hoisted up by ropes to the roof of the White Front Grill, which was across the street from City Hall.

Chief Engineer Ed Herring rented extra camera cable from NBC or somebody so it could stretch from the studio across rooftops and alleyways to the White Front. You can't do a parade with just one camera and no zoom lens. We weren't about to be able to rent another camera, but Clint somehow got us access to a rented Zoomar lens. Now this wasn't the neat, compact zoom you see today. This a ten foot long cylinder that looked more like a bazooka. It was so long, it had to be attached to the camera with guy wires. Our announcers were on the White Front Cafe roof.

In 1958 our Azalea Parade coverage was still very bare-bones and low-tech. Frank Piner mans the camera while Buck 0'Shields handles the cables. On the WECT stand, (l to r) Dallas Mills, Bill Smith & Jackie Pastis

We had to run microphone cables right along beside the camera cable. We didn't have to rent microphone cable but we used the very last inch WMFD-AM & TV had. There must have been twenty-five audio cable connectors between the studio and Third Street. In the weeks before the festival, we began to talk up the parade telecast as the first time shut-ins and people who couldn't travel to Wilmington would have a chance to see the region's premier event.

With marching bands, the Azalea Queen Sara Shane and her court, military units and floats we covered a two-hour parade and on-the-air it looked like we had been doing parades on television for years and years. We were just a bunch of radio people who didn't know you couldn't cover a parade a half block away with one studio camera and a very, very long cable.

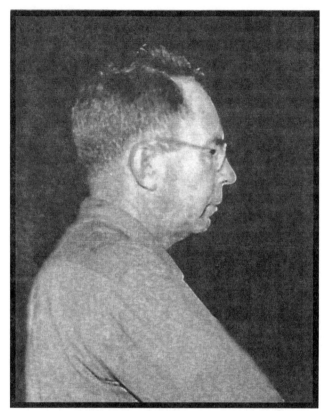

Chief Engineer Ed Herring

Chief Engineer Ed Herring's role in planning our improbable parade telecast brings to mind an incident that took place during the first few weeks we were on the air in April of 1954. The Captain and Dick Dunlea, Jr. had invited a number city and county officials and an elite group of merchants to watch our programming from the third floor studios.

They were there to see the Rhythm Range Riders and "Over At Al's" and the news, weather and sports. They were gathered in the control room as we were about to sign on at 6 o'clock, but there was something wrong. No signal of any kind was leaving our control room on the way to the transmitter on River Road in Brunswick County. We were effectively off the air. It was very embarrassing.

The Dunleas, Senior and Junior began to get very impatient as Ed Herring spread out the blueprints and schematics of the wiring on the control room floor. He got down on his hands and knees and traced each wiring connection. There must have been thousands. He pulled up the floorboards and checked every splice. Ed did not get excited, he did not seem to hurry, he was checking out everything and he was doing it methodically and thoroughly.

The Dunleas were getting more embarrassed and more impatient. They tried to hurry Ed, but he wouldn't be hurried. Finally Ed found the trouble and fixed it. The station signed on. Everybody was relieved. Ed bundled up the blueprints, re-packed his toolbox and went home. Those images of Ed Herring quietly solving the problem are what I see anytime I read that favorite poem by Rudyard Kipling.

"If you can keep your head when all about you are losing theirs and blaming it on you... "

Ed Herring kept his head and he was truly "...a Man, my son. "

Bobbie Marcroft was another of the radio people who caught on to television within a day or two. She had come to radio copywriting from a newspaper background. Another step to television was a natural. Bobbie wrote creative commercial copy, but she also developed a flair for putting words and pictures together for documentary television before the concept was widely developed.

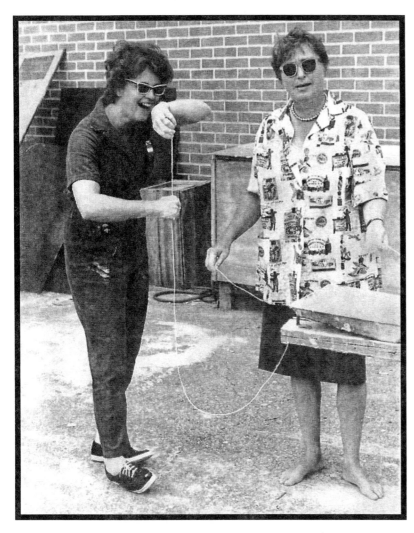

Bobbie Gurganious and Bobbie Marcroft work on a project outdoors

Within the first few months of that first year in 1954, she came up with a unique half-hour about one of Wilmington's most historic houses, the pre-Civil War Bellamy Mansion at Fifth and Market. John McNeill took a hundred still photographs and slides of the house inside and out. Bobbie and John alternated slides with stills so that with only those two video sources they could weave a seamless fabric of captivating images. Bobbie added distinctive music and a remarkable piece of early small market television was ready to be broadcast.

Then the sales department decided they could sell it. By the time the salesmen got through describing it to clients and suggesting commercial tie-ins, Bobbie and John could hardly recognize the original concept. In frustration, Bobbie coined a phrase that I have used over and over again for forty years.

"That's the last good idea I'm going to have .... here."

Of course it wasn't. She had hundreds of other good ideas that made very good television. But her frustration and the frustration of other creative people was summed up in that remark. I quoted her over the years every time somebody that hadn't had a creative idea in their entire career tried to change the creation of someone who had thousands of very good ideas.

Some very talented Channel Six people had no broadcast background of any kind. Katy Godwin had an idea for a children's program that became Kiddie Time. She also developed into an accomplished spokesperson for many southeastern North Carolina business firms. Elementary teacher Ann Dunsford brought a program idea to the station that had a strange name, but one that fitted the concept exactly. Her successful program was "Saturday Sunday School."

We took a big step up the television ladder in February of 1955 when we were interconnected and were able to carry live network programs for the first time. Before long we had The Gillette Friday Night fights, Bob Hope and John Daly and the ABC News.

One of the first live network programs we carried proved to be a test for the heartbeat of WMFD-TV. NBC presented a television adaptation of Marc Connelly's Broadway play The Green Pastures. The play is the basic Old Testament Bible story with an all black cast. God, Adam and Eve, Noah and Moses are all black. When the program began, the station switchboard started ringing and it was still ringing hours later. The calls were almost all against the telecast. In the mid 50's south-eastern North Carolina was just beginning to come out of 90 years of segregation.

It was a slow process and we believed then and still do that Channel Six was a big help in the healing. That night, no apologies were given for broadcasting the NBC adaptation. Those of us who answered the phone that night politely and carefully explained that it was a play, a very successful one that had been performed thousands of times on Broadway and also had been staged around the country during a national tour. Many callers demanded that it not be performed in Wilmington. The truth was Wilmington had joined the national art scene that night, whether it wanted to or not.

Channel Six was a community leader in offering airtime to both black and white organizations. Black churches and black schools were well represented. "Relax With Jax" plowed new ground when Wayne interviewed Walter Bess, Director of the Community Boys Club. The Williston High School Chorus sang live at Christmas time. In December 1954, Jackie Robinson — the baseball star who broke the color barrier — was in town.

The Star-News newspapers had a policy against printing the photograph of any black person. They didn't make an exception for Jackie Robinson. However, Wayne interviewed Jackie on Relax With Jax and got an excellent inter-view. We were part of the progress in race relations and we were proud of that.

Wayne Jackson interviews Baseball's Jackie Robinson
In center is Thomas Rozell, president of Black High
Schools State Sudent Councils

In the first few months of television in Wilmington we had absolutely no source of any kind for news pictures or news film so I came up with a solution that violated every copyright law but went un-detected because we were so far off the beaten television path.

To illustrate the U.S. Congress, the United Nations and almost anything else, I cut pictures out of Life magazine and pasted them on heavy cardboard and held them up to that one lone camera.

Getting any kind of news film was almost impossible so I also got a little creative. There was a public service spot for the Red Cross where President Eisenhower made a call for contributions at the end of his regular press conference. Any time Eisenhower had a press conference we ran that piece of film without the sound and I read wire copy about what he said. We also had a "Prevent Forest Fires" public service spot. It had some really neat pictures of raging forest fires. Whenever there was a fire anywhere in the country, we pulled out our trusty footage. Was it deception? Probably, but I seriously doubt we fooled anybody and it sure did put a little movement into what for a long time really was what the Captain called "picture radio."

We got called down on one incident of deception and copyright violation that was totally un-intended. We started running a second package of movies in late 1954 and Clint wanted it to have a snazzy name, a host, a set, cut-ins and look like real television. He called it Academy Award Theater.

For a set, we turned some of our rolling flats with their un-finished backsides to the camera and stenciled ACADEMY AWARD THEATER several times on the back of each flat. It looked great, but we got a very formal letter from the Academy of Motion Picture Arts and Sciences.

It said, in part: "None of the movies you are running or have the rights to run have won any Academy Awards of any kind. Please cease and desist." One of the local movie theaters had turned us in. The Academy was surely right. There was not a winner of any kind in those bad, old movies we had. Clint was quick to the rescue again. He changed the program title and the backs of the flats were re-lettered to now read ACADEMY THEATER.

No summary of what we put on the air in those early days and months would be representative without a mention of our live studio commercials. Within a few months we literally had commercials coming out our doors. The studio would sometimes be stacked up with one commercial display after the other and when one commercial was completed, that display was torn down and another put up in its place in a matter of minutes.

Commercials were two deep, side-by-side all around the studio walls and announcers would move from one to another. Were there snafus? You bet there were. Clint did a series of commercials for MacMillan and Cameron advertising vacuum cleaners. In a demonstration of its superior power, the Mac and Cam cleaner was supposed to snatch a ping-pong ball away from another brand. When Clint tried it the ball stayed with the competitor every time. He turned his vacuum on high and the other one on low and it still didn't work. He cut a good-sized hole in the hose of Brand X and the right vacuum cleaner won every time.

If there was ever any doubt of how powerful television was as a sales tool, that doubt ended in the summer of 1955. The station dreamed up a special promotion of the area as a resort and vacation destination.

1955- To prove the impact of TV advertising on sales, all on-air, sales, and studio personnel wore Bermuda shorts,starting a fashion craze for men.

Area retailers had stocked up on the shorts in anticipation of our promotion. No one ordered enough, because no one, not even Clint who dreamed up the promotion, had any idea how successful it would be.

I am convinced that we made Bermuda Shorts fashionable for men in coastal North and South Carolina. We all looked dumb at first because we were required to wear the high socks. Then someone started wearing regular short socks and everybody felt a lot more comfortable. The sales power of Channel Six was proven once again.

Despite all this success, we were told the station wasn't making any money and we couldn't buy any of the equipment we so badly needed to be able to do our job. We were even told we could not buy any material for sets and we could not buy any props. We needed a simple tall wooden bar stool for a new program. We were told we couldn't buy one. Jaybird Merritt, one of our most creative studio cameramen, went to the Reno Pool Room on Second Street and shot three games of eight-ball with the owner and won a bar stool.

Jaybird was also the centerpiece of one of the funniest incidents I have ever seen in a TV studio. George Tregembo of the Tote-Em-In Zoo on Carolina Beach Road came to the studios once a week to host a program built around an animal film series we bought. He would bring up small animals, birds and almost always snakes.

One night a rattlesnake got away from George and fell to the studio floor and headed straight for our one camera and our one camera operator, Jaybird Merritt. To say Jaybird was afraid of snakes is to minimize the problem. He was terrified, but had composure enough to lock the camera in a stationary position before he ran down the three flights of steps and didn't stop running until he was safe on Princess Street three floors below.

Of course, everybody in the studio, the control room and all over the station broke up and it was hard to bring any kind of normalcy to the program that night. I'm not sure what normal television production was those first three years. We were all radio people and we were making it up as we went along.

By the summer of 1957 we were broadcasting 18 hours a day and were transmitting with full power from a new tall tower. "Hello" Myrtle Beach and northeastern South Carolina. By now all of us had three years of TV experience. We still weren't a real TV station, because of that one camera, but we were getting closer. Ownership would change in October. I left the station to pursue a boyhood dream of announcing for the 50,000-watt radio voice of Eastern North Carolina, WPTF in Raleigh.

I came back to my hometown and Channel Six in 1960. By then the station had new call letters, WECT. There was a new, one-story building on Shipyard Boulevard designed especially for television and that all-important second studio camera. Did it mean we had arrived in television's Promised Land? Not hardly.

The Channel Six I returned to in 1960 was much different from the TV station I two years earlier. All original members of that top-rated announcing staff had left for other pastures. Clint Long had gone into sales in Charlotte. He would succumb to a fatal illness in 1962. Clint was 36.

Former Wilmington Mayor Dan Cameron now headed the ownership. He brought years of success in a variety of business enterprises. There were also out-of-town elements in the ownership, some involved in the ownership of WNCT in Greenville, North Carolina, and responsible, we were told, for the selection of WECT as the call letters.

With two studios cameras and the ability to move one or both of them out of the station, we were able to continue the Channel Six tradition of live coverage of significant events.

In October of 1960, the North Carolina Highway Commission held an all day public hearing on the pros and cons of building a high level bridge over the Cape Fear River. Never had such a hearing been televised live. WECT broke precedent and opened the process to viewers throughout southeastern North Carolina.

The bridge question had dominated public debate for months.

Another First...... Our First Live Televised Public Hearing

Two of the better quotes included, "Before there is a high level bridge over the Cape Fear River there will be major league baseball on the Outer Banks." Hatteras 3, Yankees 2. The Dodgers 6, Ocracoke 1." and "There will be an American on the moon before there will be a high level bridge in Wilmington." He was right.

I came back to Wilmington as production manager and also continued air work as both a newscaster and a commercial spokesman. Commercials were a whole lot easier with two cameras and so was everything else. Despite the technical improvements, we were still the 128th market in the country and our ad rates didn't support some of the things we really needed.

The networks would not pay line charges to Wilmington, so the station had constructed its own microwave transmission system from the Greenville-Washington market to bring live programs from all three networks. Microwave systems were not as dependable as they would be later and ours had to be shut down for improvements and maintenance some part of almost every day.

When the system was out we had to pick up a live over-the-air signal from Greenville or Washington. The picture was often snowy and it tended to fade in and out. When this happened the control room was forced to put up a trouble slide and have the booth announcer say:

"The trouble you are experiencing is not in your receiver. Technicians are working to correct the trouble."

A. lot of these outages occurred in the afternoons during the very popular CBS daytime dramas, Guiding Light, As The World Turns and The Edge of Night. Angry viewers took out their frustration by giving WECT a slogan it didn't want. "We Experience Constant Trouble." WMFD had stood for "We Make Friends Daily" and WECT was simply "We're Eastern Carolina Television." The Constant Trouble label was certainly un-welcome, but it may have been deserved. The microwave mess was a necessary evil for a long time.

We no longer cut pictures out of Life magazine for our newscasts, but we had no film or tape news service and no UP fax pictures. Both were standard fare at larger stations. Both were standard fare at our sister-station WNCT in Greenville. We felt more like a stepsister. When our engineers went to Greenville to work on the micro-wave they would sometimes bring me back a stack of outdated, faded fax news pictures they had taken out of the WNCT trash basket. Did we feel second rate? In that case, we certainly did. It hurt. It was just another challenge, "do more with less."

Somehow that seemed the small market curse of Channel Six, despite all the spectacular improvements in only six years.

We beat that curse with another bit of television sleight-of-hand. Because we carried CBS afternoon programming from 1:30 to 5 o'clock, the feed was still up when that network sent its affiliates a closed circuit broadcast of filmed news stories not being used on the CBS Evening News. CBS affiliates paid for this service. We were an NBC affiliate. We shoplifted the CBS 5 o'clock News feed and it was a very long time before anybody stopped us. If you paid for the service, you got scripts for the silent film stories on your CBS Teletype. One or two staff announcers in New York would read some of the scripts under the film, just to help stations match up the narration. Those voices were never supposed to be used on the air. It was against union rules, and "the first amendment to the Bible" as a Texas friend of mine used to say.

We used those voices whenever we could. Since they were never identified, we started giving them made-up names to fit where the story was coming from. I had some real tongue-in-cheek fun with the names. I could call in Sean Goldstein from Israel or Moses O'Grady from Northern Ireland and Pierre Sanchez from Mexico City. Was it deception? Probably. It was that small-market curse again. You can't do a national newscast without any pictures or any news film. You can't? We didn't know that and we did it anyway.

We continued to do as many live broadcasts of local events as we could. One I especially remember was the telecast of a Junior College regional tournament game from Brogden Hall. It was the first basketball game we had televised and we would show off our two cameras. The General Manager wanted us to put one camera on one side of the court and one on the other.

"That way people on both sides of the gym will see our cameras."

Wayne and I tried to reason that when we switched cameras on a fast break, the players who had been running from left to right would now we running right to left. I don't think we ever convinced the GM, but so many staff members agreed with our reasoning that he let us set up the cameras the way we wanted to. We had some of that old Channel Six blind luck during that remote. The very close game ended in a player fight and a fan riot caused by Seahawk player Neil Johnson, who later had a professional career at Philadelphia of the NBA and the Virginia Squires of the ABA.

First Local Basketball TeleCast ..... Cameramen Dallas Mills and
Buck O'Shields, and announcer Wayne Jackson

Bringing Home
Our Battleship

In 1960 and '61 we devoted a lot of attention to Wilmington's successful bid to bring the Battleship North Carolina to the Cape Fear River as a World War II Memorial. The idea was originated in the local American Legion Post by legionnaire and WECT account executive Jimmy Craig. Channel Six led fund-raising with a statewide telecast.

Far left, Hugh Morton, Committee Chairman,
Second from right, Jimmy Craig, WECT Sales Rep

John McNeill and I went to Bayonne, New Jersey where the battleship was docked as state and local officials accepted the ship from the Navy.

Tugboats begin to push the USS North Carolina into its new berth.

The ship was towed into the Wilmington harbor in October of 1961, but neither Jimmy Craig nor John McNeill was there to see it. They would lose their lives in a plane crash as part of the WECT Air Show a month earlier.

That tragedy changed forever my personal remembrances of Channel Six. Memories that had been "terrific" were replaced by memories that were "tragic." I know the crash changed me, and it changed the station.

John and Jimmy and account executive C.D. Martin were aboard a military plane taking off from the runway at New Hanover County Airport to carry the elite Airborne parachute team, The Golden Knights, to the proper altitude for their sky diving demonstration.

The transport plane crashed on takeoff. We were televising live and I was the director. We had a close-up shot of the plane on the air when it hit the end of the runway and burst into flames. It was several minutes before someone told me our folks were on the plane.

It was almost impossible for me to keep my composure. Jimmy and C.D. were good friends; John McNeill was the best friend I ever had. We started at Channel Six together in 1954, becoming Hurricane Hazel veterans. Both of us left for a time, John to WITN in Washington, North Carolina and me to Raleigh, but we had looked forward to working together again. Jimmy Craig died 3 weeks after the crash, John died a month later at the U.S. Army Burn Center at Fort Sam Houston, Texas.

After a painful recovery, C.D. survived and returned to a successful sales and management career. The crash also cost the lives of 3 members of the military. It was the last of the WECT Air Shows, which began in 1958 and had grown to be the biggest of its kind in the country. It was also the last of the days of TV Camelot for many members of the original staff and for me. There is a plaque on the lobby wall at WECT, a permanent memorial to Jimmy Craig and John McNeill.

John T. McNeill, III

IN MEMORY OF
JAMES S. CRAIG, JR.
ACCOUNT EXECUTIVE

JOHN T. McNEILL, III
DIRECTOR OF PHOTOGRAPHY

DIED FROM INJURIES
SUSTAINED DURING
4TH ANNUAL
W E C T
C.A.P. AIR SHOW

SEPTEMBER 24, 1961

James S. Craig, Jr.

In April 1964 we had 10 candles of our birthday cake. The programming and sales departments noted that on April 9, 1954 WMFD-TV was on the air 5 hours and broadcast 12 commercials. On April 9, 1964, WECT had 18 hours of programming and 215 commercials. "Picture Radio" had become a real television station.

Jim Burns lights candles on our tenth birthday cake as Wayne Jackson, (left), WECT President Dan Cameron and Jane Rhett look on.

By the summer of 1964, I was certain my future was in TV News, but not in a small market. Stations in the bigger markets were establishing journalism-based news departments.

I wrote to a dozen stations in the top 50 markets in the southeastern states. I only applied to the top station in each city. I really wanted to be part of a first class operation in a top market. In September I joined the news staff at WTAR-TV in Norfolk, Virginia. The pioneer TV station was owned by one of the most respected newspapers in the south and Channel Three was the top rated CBS affiliate in the country.

I was thirty-one years old and ending the first ten years of a television career that would span 44 years. I had learned a lot. We all had. It was quite a ride for the group that began WMFD-TV. We had all been radio people. Not any more.

An unknown crew member drew this wimsical layout of the old downtown studio. Notice the back-to-back sets for the various live shows lined closely along the back wall, so that the only camera could be quickly rolled from one to another. Some of the crew seem to having a few problems.

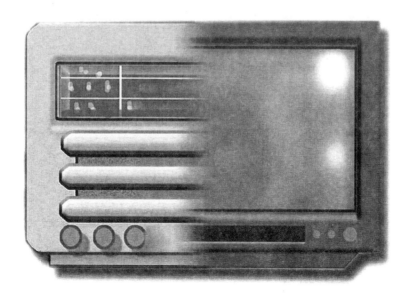

TV6... WMFD-TV - WECT
THE EARLY YEARS
by Wayne Jackson

When I accepted an offer to begin a television career by hosting a brand new afternoon talk show, never did I believe it would lead to a career lasting almost 35 years, all in Wilmington. "Relax With Jax" premiered September 27, 1954 and ran for a very long hour and 25 minutes ...4:30-5:55pm. I say very long because it was all live, all in the studio with one camera, no television experience and little idea of what a challenging project we had started.

Ideas and people come together in many ways. WMFD-TV had started operating April 9, 1954, with a daily schedule of programs starting at 6:00pm and ending about 10:30pm. There was no live network and all programs were either live in the studio or on film. Those in charge wanted to expand the telecast day and decided to originate a live local program. In my radio days in Rocky Mount I had come to know some of the staff people at WMFD and they came forward and offered me the opportunity to host the program. My wife, Lee, and I discussed this at some length and finally decided this would be a good move and I would get involved with the young television industry. With two young sons, the move was a family affair, not just a change in my work schedule. The entire Jackson family was embarking on a new adventure.

Before going in front of the camera I had to spruce my wardrobe. On radio, sitting in the control room all by yourself, jeans and a sport shirt was plenty of dress, but on television, in front of the camera and going into peoples homes, you needed to look better. So I was introduced to Mr. Harry Payne at his Payne's Men's Store and he fixed me up with a suit, couple of sport coats, slacks, shirts and ties so I would be presentable to viewers. The cost and payment? The cost has long been forgotten ... the payment was a handshake and pay me as you can. No check...no credit card ... no bill to sign. Just "welcome to Wilmington and I'll be watching you". I was overwhelmed by his courtesy and trust.

P.S. Mr. Payne was paid back and my credit was good.

The first program aired just a few days after I arrived in Wilmington. And as I knew almost nothing about Wilmington and the people in town, Bob West, Clint Long and others had contacted people and lined up the guests for the first two weeks or so. Bob worked as producer of the program ...Clint Long was the program director and also did the weather forecasts in the newscasts.

The initial guest was very prestigious .... U.S. Senator Alton Lennon, who was a Wilmingtonian. What a great way that was to introduce a new program to our television audience.

Our guests came from all walks of life ... elected officials, high school cheerleaders, garden clubs, veterans organizations and from Wilmington and surrounding counties as we worked to branch out to friends in the whole coverage area.

We were a local station, owned and operated by a Wilmington broadcast pioneer, R.A. Dunlea, Sr. and he often said..."we will serve our local area and the wonderful people who live here".

(L to R) R. A. Dunlea, Jr., General Manager, Clint Long, Program director and
R.A. Dunlea, Sr., president and founder of WMFD-TV

This same theme was echoed by the succeeding owner ... Dan Cameron and his partners. We would be an integral part of our entire coverage area. This was enjoyable and not difficult, as the people, history and culture of the area provided unlimited sources of interesting and informative programs. More on that later.

Our studio was on the third floor of a building on Princess St. and there was no elevator so guests had a good climb to get up to where the action was. It also presented a challenge for sponsors who wanted to display items on their commercials. For instance, if a refrigerator was to be featured someone had to put it on a dolly and get it up to the third floor ... step by step.

Buck O'Shields looks on as Engineer Mike Loizides checks the camera controls during the station's early days

We hit a high note on "Relax With Jax" on December 2, 1954, when our guest was baseball hall-of-famer Jackie Robinson. He was in Wilmington to speak to a meeting of high school student council members from black high schools in North Carolina. The meeting was held at Williston High School. With Robinson was Thomas Rozell, president of the state student council association. Just a few days later the Williston Concert Choir appeared on the program and presented an outstanding program of Christmas holiday tunes. They were sensational and came back in the spring for a second performance.

The choir was directed by Ms. Constance O'Dell. These appearances were quite noteworthy as in the segregated society of 1954 the black community did not get much publicity or notice other than the black weekly paper, the Wilmington Journal. Some years later the Williston alumni recognized me for my "Pioneering Spirit". But this was all part of the goal to serve the entire community as espoused by Mr. Dunlea and Mr. Cameron.

The man running our one and only black and white camera faced quite a challenge. He had to move from a single shot of me to a wider shot of me and the guest, or guests, and still stay in focus and not jiggle the camera and picture up and down. Harold Ludwig and Roland Heustess became experts at this.

We also had a bulletin board setup next to the set with posters and announcements of community events displayed on the board. When I mentioned activities in the area, a slide would be inserted in the control room so the camera could move and focus on the bulletins. I would then read from the posters while the camera focused on them and the camera would smoothly go from poster to poster without losing focus. It was a special ability that Harold and Roland mastered.

The lengthy "Relax With Jax" did not have a long run, as the program schedule changed considerably February 18, 1955, when live NBC network programs became available. Afternoon programs started at 3:00pm with the soap opera "The Greatest Gift". Local and NBC programs alternated from 3:00-6:00 and our program log looked like this:

3:00	The Greatest Gift, NBC
3:15	Relax With Jax
3:30	One Man's Family, NBC
3:45	Relax With Jax
4:00	Hawkins Falls, NBC
4:15	Relax With Jax
4:45	Kiddie Time, local childrens program
5:00	Pinky Lee, NBC
5:30	Howdy Doody, NBC

"Kiddie Time" was an exceptional program. Katherine Godwin, housewife and mother, came to Mr. Dunlea with the idea to produce a daily children's program. Again, great plans, absolutely no experience, but undeniable desire and an attitude that made us all believe she would succeed. So Mr. Dunlea gave his okay and another local live program came to life. Katy (we didn't call her Katherine) was a winner from the start. The kids loved her and she had no problems getting guests. Her shows were educational, entertaining, humorous, full of

Katy Godwin's "Kiddie Time" brought children flocking to the station where they became a part of the show

wisdom and participants and viewers of Kiddie Time were well-rewarded for spending time with Katy. As with other local programs, Kiddie Time varied in length at different times and also came on different times as the schedule varied through the months and years. And with live programs you were at the mercy of people appearing with you. On one program she asked a young boy who his father was and he replied.. "I don't know". Katy blushed and moved on quickly, while the control room went into an uproar ... the boy's father was standing right there watching the studio show.

The first local programs, other than news, sports and weather, began when the station signed on April 9, 1954. "Over at Al's" was a musical and fun program hosted by Al Compton, with a musical cast of Bob and Fred Hickman, Tex Lancaster and beautiful blond songstress Twiddle. Comical bits came from "Hayseed" formally known as C.O. Thomas.

The Rhythm Range Riders, on their log cabin set, were featured on the live show"Over at Al's" Shown L to R are Tex Lancaster, Bob and Freddie Hickman, "Twiddle" McConkey, C.O. "Hayseed" Thomas, and host Al Compton

This was a nightly that kicked off the evening at 6:OOpm, Monday - Saturday. "TV Song Shop" was a featured live studio program each evening .... hosted by Clay McBride and Bob Caudle.. who would be like a radio deejay, talking it up and then placing a needle on a spinning record and then a tune on film would come up on the TV sets at home.

Announcer Clay McBride hosted a DJ style music show against a backdrop of album covers, sometimes resorting to camera shots of the records spinning arond.

"Bob and Hester" was not on nightly, but was a regular program featuring Bob Caudle and Stan Rehder, a local man with a great sense of humor. Stan would sit under the desk and hold up a puppet. "Hester" and he and Bob would hold conversations on whatever crazy subject they could dream up. It was funny and quite popular. And there was "Western Theater", one of very popular programs with young and old. John Thomas, a recent New Hanover High School graduate, was dubbed "Johnny Ranger", and he was host of the program. John was dressed as a cowboy and just a knockout for the hour long film program. John was also an excellent pianist and played in bands and for special occasions.

All of these men had long and distinguished careers, mostly in broadcasting. Al Compton became a Baptist missionary and then a top person in the Southern Baptist Radio and TV commission. A year or so later Bill Weathers, hosted a Saturday "Top Ten Dance Party", with Bill as a d.j. and couples coming up to dance the Saturday away.

George Tregembo, owner of the Tote-Em-In Zoo, would appear as the live, local segment of a program we called "Safari". I was on with George most of the time and we began the half hour with a few minutes discussion of some wild animal he had at the zoo ... then came a 15 minute film about

Africa and animals, then we concluded with more talk from George and anything he may have brought with him. There were so many other local live studio programs.

Jane Rhett showed viewers that "Cooking Can Be Fun" as she whipped up daily recipes and meals in our studio. The staff ate heartily each afternoon after Jane signed off.

Ann Dunsford came up with her original program ..."Saturday Sunday School" with children as her guests. A very successful program and one that taught her participants how to be better people. Dallas Mills was behind the camera for most of her programs. Ann and Dallas married and Ann continued her time with children by becoming a first grade teacher.

Ben McDonald originated "Carolina Farm Beat", an early morning program, complete with down home music, farm news and local guests Ben later had a news show and with his tip of "my old and battered homburg" and BMF magic hair formula became a much talked-about character. George Deaton succeeded Ben on the "Farm Beat" show.

The single longest running local program was the "Jim Burns Show". Jim, a local guy, joined the staff in 1958 and his live program followed. His half hour presentation ran for over 20 years and his guests filled the studio for 52 weeks every year. For many years Jim also presented the weather on the early news programs.

In the 50s our coverage area was still largely rural, so Ben McDonald's farm report was popular

Combining the local news, sports and weather with live commercials was one of our most difficult tasks. With little visual material to work with, careful planning was of the utmost necessity. On a good commercial day, two live commercials would be set up on either side of the news desk, two more next to sports and two next to weather. At a break in the news, a slide of the sponsor would flash up and the camera would quickly move to the commercial.

After that announcer finished selling his product a sponsor slide would again go up and the camera would move over to the next commercial setup. A sponsor slide would be shown for about ten seconds at the end of that sales pitch so the camera could move back to the news set. That maneuver would be repeated following the news, then the sports and finally the weather. Announcers could have sold refrigerators, tires, clothing, books, fishing equipment, food, bicycles and cameras in the commercials ... all live and on camera.

When announcers were to do live commercials, we would go to the sponsor and discuss the product to be sold , go over the possible script and sometimes take the props back to the station. With no teleprompter on the camera to show the script, most times we would make notes on a large piece of paper or card, clip it on the side of the camera and ad lib the commercial. If you did the same commercial several times you could almost memorize the entire script. After a while, doing commercials for the same sponsor became much easier as we gained confidence with each other. A few of my accounts were Foy Roe & Co., a men's store, DE Dodge and Godwin Lumber & Oil Co.

We were paid a talent fee, something like a dollar, for each commercial and if we messed up and the sponsor was dissatisfied with our presentation, we would have to come back in a night or two to do a make-good commercial with no compensation. That was incentive enough to do a good commercial the first time.

To protect sponsors from competitors, commercials for like products were placed at least 15 minutes apart. If a Chevrolet dealer had a commercial at 6:15, no other automobile dealer would run a commercial before 6:30. We didn't have a great many sponsors at first so that was no problem. In later years the protection time dropped to five minutes and now it's not unusual to see competitors run back-to-back during the same break.

Many commercials consisted of slides with an announcer reading the copy from the audio booth. The men in the film room always told the directors to check the slides before the commercials were to run to be sure everything was loaded and in the proper order. Some directors did not always do that, and one night during a spot for an auto dealer, an unusual slide came on air. Instead of an automobile, the slide said this... "Feed 'em Doughnuts". The director was shocked and took the screen to black, the announcer did not know what to say and after a few seconds the director put a film on the air. The man in the film department had made his point, and the sponsor received a make-good commercial. The director went back to checking his slides.

Selling television could be difficult in the first years..... we weren't on the air all day and night, there were few sets, we had no live network until February 1955 and the new kid on the block had to prove itself. Working together, gaining experience and confidence and showing a willingness to be bold and innovative with local programming enabled us to improve rapidly.

At one time in the following years, during what I think was a national sales week, sales people reminded us that "Nothing Happens Until a Sale is Made".... the counter to that was.. "No Sale is Made Until a Product is Produced".

The growth of the daily program schedule and our sales ability was pointed out when WECT celebrated our tenth anniversary in 1964.. Our program said ... April 9, 1954, 5 Hours, 12 Commercials ..... April 9, 1964, 18.5 Hours, 215 Commercials.

The early newscasts were plain and simple. We had one black and white camera, some silent film and photographs but no sound-on-film or videotape, no satellite trucks for remote news stories. Three white males at three desks did news, sports and weather. There was no chit chat between the three, no Dopplers and all the various things on today's weather shows.

We did read some national news because we had no live network, but as soon as we started getting network news we just did local and state news, using our local sources and clips from the Associated Press news wire. Our weather board was a blackboard, like those in schools, with the U.S. outlined in yellow paint, and North Carolina outlined the same way.

Cameraman Dallas Mills checks the script while staffers prepare for Ben McDonald's nightly news show

41

Below that was a smaller board with space for temperatures etc. Frontal systems, high and low pressure areas and temperatures were all written in with chalk. The information written in chalk for the early news was erased so the new weather data could be written for the late news. Clint Long, who reported the weather, would call the weather bureau for facts and figures and also get some information from the A.P. news wire. Primitive ...yes. .but it worked and we worked hard to get it right. Remember, television was very young ... everyone was searching for the best way to inform the viewer.

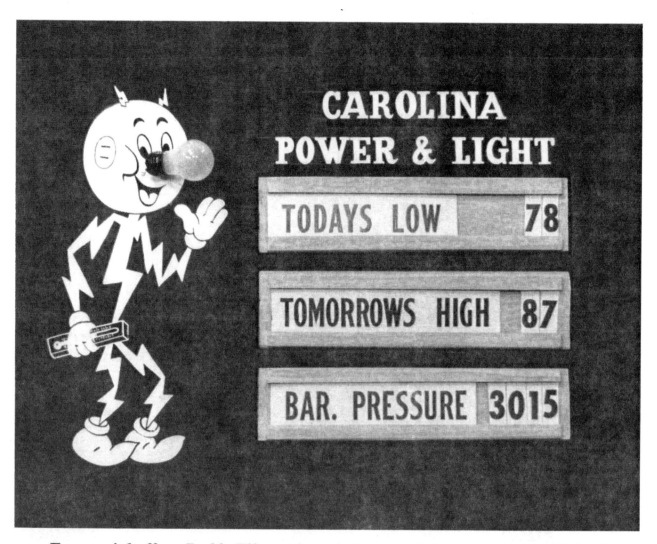

For special effect, Reddy Kilowatt's nose lit up as the weather board showed the day's highs and lows. The board was created by staff artist Bebe Bryant

Since we had no videotape to record the news programs and check our work, we relied on each other. Nightly critique sessions were held and we discussed our work in a very frank and forthright manner. It's easy to get into habits of using certain words and phrases over and over. These sessions could stop that.

Another item we looked at was our relationship to the viewer. We felt that when someone at home turned on the TV set to watch us, it was as though they were inviting us a guest into their home, and we should relate to that and be a guest ... friendly and factual.

We also wanted to be aware of how we presented the news and how voice inflection, emphasis on certain words, eyes widen or roll, body language can all give an editorial impression of how the news is being given. This has not changed through the years. See if you can pick it up when watching the news.

One of the most interesting aspects of our local news was the ability of Bob West to memorize his newscast and look right into the camera and present the news with no cue card. He was amazing!!!

While the in-studio work was interesting, a whole new world opened up when we began to think of going outside the studio to broaden our efforts. The idea of man-on-the-street interviews came up for our Relax with Jax program. Engineering said it was possible to take the camera and break it into two parts, the main body and the undercarriage, take it down to the street, drop camera and microphone cables from the third floor to the street and then hook it all back up. This could be done in about ten minutes, so one day we introduced a 15 minute film, got the camera and cables down to Princess St., hooked it all up and when the film finished there we were ... camera and microphone ... waiting to stop and talk with anyone passing by who might agree to chat with us. Most people stopped but some quickly crossed the street before they got to our location.

Two advances in programming made the end of the first year of WMFD-TV special. In February, 1955, the very first live network programs were added to the schedule. On Friday, February 18, 1955 afternoon serials and children's programs came to the viewers along with The Life of Riley, Gillette Cavalcade of Sports and the Jan Murray Show in the evening. The daytime serials were The Greatest Gift, One Man's Family and Hawkins Falls. For the children, Pinky Lee and Howdy Doody filled the bill. All were NBC network programs.

The second program move was the decision to televise the Azalea Festival parade, live from beginning to end. This was a daring decision in light of our very modest equipment and no experience. Before we look further at special remote programs, I will continue with the expansion of our program day.

In October 1956 WMFD TV brought morning TV to Wilmington. Love of Life at 11:15 and Guiding Light at 11:45 started the day as CBS programs became available. The afternoon was a mixture of NBC, CBS and local programs. Tennessee Ernie, Matinee Theater, Stand Up and Be Counted and Comedy Time were NBC programs. Brighter Day, Secret Storm and Edge of Night came from CBS and Cooking Can Be Fun and Kiddie Time originated from our studio.

7:OOAM was sign on time June 3, 1957 when the two hour Today show came from NBC. Also that day Home and The Price is Right came from NBC and Strike It Rich was added from CBS.

For a few years we carried programs from all three networks.. NBC, CBS and ABC. ABC was dropped early in 1964 when it was announced that WWAY would be an ABC affiliate upon coming on the air later that year.

There were changes off the air also ... in October 1957, ownership was taken over by Dan and Bruce Cameron and their partners and the new corporation became Atlantic Telecasting Corporation. Mr. Dunlea had started TV in Wilmington and moved it forward in rapid fashion and now he would continue with his successful radio station. One of the partners in the new ownership was Roy Park, who also owned WNCT-TV in Greenville.

Network shows in color began in December 1957..new call letters WECT replaced WMFD-TV in February 1958 and later in 1958 a station owned micro-wave relay system went into operation to bring network programs into town.

The moving van loads for the move to WECT's new home on Shipyard Blvd.

In April 1959, we moved from our third floor studios in downtown Wilmington to a new building on Shipyard Blvd. That old Princess St. building has since been torn down.

WECT staffers had a going away party at the Ambassador Coffee Shop before leaving downtown. The new studios were expanded in 1962 to house two big RCA video tape units and another expansion in 1967 made room for a new lobby, 10 offices, another studio and more storage space. In 1968 two color studio cameras went into operation and our local studio programs were seen in color for the first time. WECT went public with stock in 1972 and thousands of shares were sold in a few days.

There were tears, and grins, at the Ambassador Coffee Shop as the station left downtown. L to R: Jack Forehand,Frank Piner, Faith Buchanan, Betsy Everett. Lower rt.corner, Bobbie Marcroft and Wayne Jackson

To expand the viewing area, a 1,000 foot tower was put up in Delco and with full power our programs reached a much larger area. Then in 1969 construction was completed on a 2,000 foot tower near White Lake in Bladen County which doubled our coverage area and enabled us to reach hundreds of thousands of new viewers. We had a contest at that time and the winner was a couple from Fayetteville. Their prize was a ride in the elevator to the top of the tower. They said they really enjoyed the trip!

The completion of the 2,000 foot tower also brought a change in station ownership. With a much broader coverage area, our signal had significant overlap with the signal of WNCT-TV in Greenville, N.C. With someone having ownership in both stations it created what the Federal Com-

1969 - Our new 2000 foot tower at White Lake was the tallest man-made structure east of the Mississippi

munications Commission a "duopoly" and Mr. Park and his partners at WNCT had to sell their part ownership in WECT. The stations were competing for viewers in several counties in eastern North Carolina.

As that first year of television came to an end, a birthday party was held with the cake cut by our Pres., Mr. R.A. Dunlea, Sr. He was joined at the cake table by his son, Dick Dunlea, Jr., chief engineer Ed Herring, secretary Julie Mae Mitton and sales manager Claud O'Shields. Then we all had a piece of cake and looked forward to the coming year.

WMFD-TV was one year old in April, 1955-Enjoying the party are
L to R, Dick Dunlea, Jr., Gen. Mgr., R.A Dunlea Sr., Chief Engineer
Ed Herring, Secretary Julie Mae Mitton, & Claud O'Shields, Sales Mgr..

That year began with a bang ... our first telecast of the Azalea Festival parade. Chief engineer Ed Herring came up with enough camera and microphone cable that we were able to stretch it from our third floor location on Princess St. out the window and to the White Front Grill which was on Third St. right across from City Hall and the reviewing stand. A zoom lens was rented for the camera so we could get close-ups of the parade units. Announcers were on top of the restaurant. With only the one camera it was tricky to follow a parade unit from right to left down the parade route and then swing back to pick up the next unit. It was not fancy, it was simple, but it worked and we were ecstatic that we had done it and that started years of televising the parade. Soon we were able to use wireless microphones and roam the street and reviewing stand talking to various marchers and people along the route.

A few years later we had our own remote bus unit to use for remote telecasts, and we also built a two-level stand on which we put our camera on top and on the lower level we had room for family to sit and watch the parade. All aspects of the telecasts were upgraded as the years went by. It was a simple start that only got better and better.

The parade telecasts led to our involvement with the Azalea Festival regarding celebrity guests. We were asked to aid the festival in getting television celebrities to be part of the annual event. As westerns were very popular in the 1950s and 1960s we worked in that direction. Dale Robertson, star of NBC's Wells Fargo came in 1957, Wayde Preston of Colt 45 was parade marshal in 1960, Nick Adams from The Rebel came in 1961 and probably the most popular star of that time, Michael Landon, of NBC's Bonanza, was parade marshal in 1964.

Azalea Festival celebrity James Drury, star of "The Virginian", poses for photos with L toR. Dot Romeo, Gwen Todd, Cornelia Leeuwenburg, Bebe Braynt & Hattie Squires. In front are Elsie Reed, Bobbie Gurganious and Jackie Pastis

Pete Capps, festival president in 1961, called the station with an urgent plea .... get me an innocent, young lady to be our queen. A large newspaper in the state evidently ran an article referring to the Azalea Festival as several days of booze, bosoms and broads. Mr. Capps wanted to change that. After several calls we were able to give Mr. Capps some very good news. Shelley Fabares, who was starring in the "Donna Reed Show", would be Queen Azalea in 1961. Miss Fabares was 19 or 20, and came with her mother and the press agent for the company which produced the program.

A few other queens we worked with NBC to come to the festival were Whitney Blake from "Hazel", Abby Dalton from the "Joey Bishop Show", and Patricia Blair from "Daniel Boone".

In 1972 we were very fortunate to make arrangements for Demond Wilson, starring in "Sanford and Son" to appear in the festival.

1961 was the year that John Larkin, starring in the afternoon serial "The Edge of Night" agreed to be a guest. As Mike Karr, he played one of the good guys on the show. When the word got out that one of Edge of Night stars was coming to Wilmington, we received a phone call at the station from an elderly lady who thought one of the bad guys on the program was to be here.

She said, in so many words, "we don't want anyone like that in Wilmington. He is awful and if he comes he may not leave alive". We assured the caller that she would be happy with the guest. Showing the popularity of afternoon soap operas, and especially John Larkin, he was overwhelmed by people wherever he went. He had a police escort, people at the parade gave him standing ovations and he could hardly believe it. This had been his first personal appearance and he had no idea of his popularity. I heard that he made a second appearance somewhere in the midwest and the response was the same so he bowed out of the afternoon television business and headed to Hollywood to further his career.

NBC was very helpful and cooperative, especially after the festival committee invited the press agent to come as a guest and enjoy four days of Wilmington hospitality. He had a ball and was always available anytime I called him after that visit.

WECT people also worked in various capacities with various ;'festival committees. A 1964 Coronation Show and Pageant program listed Jimmy Moore and Bebe Bryant as furnishing art work, and Jackie Pastis as coordinator for the 38 queens who were hostesses. Bobbie Marcroft of the WECT staff worked on several pageants and aided the committee in numerous ways.

POLITICS

The first political advertisement listed on a log was a 15 minute program for a Seavy Carroll, candidate for Congress which ran April 30, 1954, at 8:15 PM. This was listed as a live presentation from the studio. No one on the staff at that time has any memory of Mr. Carroll or his candidacy.

Political ads were either done live in the studio or were read over slides. Most were live and done in many unique ways as none of the candidates had ever appeared in front of a camera before coming into the studio. One local candidate wanted 15 minutes for his talk but we urged him to take a 5 minute period instead. We knew him and doubted he could handle 15 minutes. He insisted on 15 minutes...it was his money so his decision was final. The evening he sat down in front of the camera turned into somewhat of a learning experience for everyone.

The man read his entire talk in just 6 minutes and when he got a signal indicating he had 9 minutes to go, he reread his entire copy. Upon receiving a cue showing him that he still had 3 minutes remaining, he just said 'That's all I have to say. Vote for me.... and the station can have the rest of my time."

We were prepared and had loaded two films of public service announcements which then ran.

The man said to us later..."I had no idea 15 minutes was such a long time."

Political ads in the 50s concluded with the disclaimer.. "This was a paid political announcement". No names as to who paid for the spot. We would get calls from some regular advertisers at times and they would say.. I have a commercial running at 8:OO pm, Give that time to ....and they would tell us what candidate would show up to talk. After the political minute we would announce.. "this was a paid political announcement" with no mention of the sponsor.

This came to an end when the rule passed that all political announcements must say who paid for it. As an example-if an auto dealer wanted to give a candidate his time we would have to announce that   ... Automotive company paid for the commercial. No company wanted to be associated with any candidate for fear of creating ill will among their customers so they stopped giving their time away.

Local candidate George Rountree had a simple way of ending his announcements by just saying.. "This was a paid political announcement and I paid for it."

A station cannot censor a candidate and cannot be held liable for anything they say. However, if some one speaks on behalf of a candidate the station could be held liable for what they say. We never had a serious problem with the rules.

While we would not censor an ad, we would sometimes express an opinion as to its content. For example ... one local man wanted to show his disdain for an opponents statements in this way. He said.. "This is what I think of my opponents platform..': and then he slowly let the air out of a balloon, creating a unique sound. We questioned the wisdom of this but he insisted it was what he wanted. The spot ran a few nights later and about 15 minutes after it aired the man called me at home and said..."don't run it again ... my wife is furious with me." End of story.

Equal time provisions were always something to be aware of. If a candidate was interviewed for a news story equal time was not an issue. But if a candidate appeared on a local talk show his opponents would be able to claim and discuss whatever they wanted to talk about. Gil Burnett was on Jim Burns program one day to discuss sail boats.. no mention of Burnett running for office, although he was a candidate. His opponent, George Clark, called and wanted time to discuss his political views. Then he laughed and withdrew his claim for time but wanted us to know he was watching and that he had a valid claim.

During the years ballots in elections were counted by hand, we were often on air until well past midnight. One time, about 3:00am, we remarked ...I wonder if anyone is still up and watching us? The phone rang with local calls and also from Lumberton, Southport and elsewhere.

Once or twice there were statewide returns from Raleigh. A network of 5 or 6 stations would band together, each sending a reporter or two to Raleigh, and all stations would then get up-to-the-minute results of statewide races. Cutaways would be set in the format so we could all report on our local races. WRAL-TV was the driving force behind this.

In 1960 a call from local attorney John Burney led to a political first in North Carolina ..... a live, local, 30 minute rally for a candidate. The man was Dr. I. Beverly Lake, running for governor in the Democratic primary. Mr. Burney asked if we could televise a program from the county courthouse ... paid for by the Lake for Governor committee. We had never done this ... and calls to other television stations in the state told us that no one had ever done this. Their reaction was..."You want to do what? That's crazy".

Crazy or not, we sat down with John ... he showed us his plan .... our technical staff said it could be done ... so we did it.

The thirty minute program started at 8:00pm with a short announcement and then a roomful of shouting Lake supporters making joyful sounds. John Burney appeared to stir up the crowd even more and introduced Dr. Lake at which time the courtroom noise level jumped to its highest level. We had told all participants that they had to conclude by 8:29 for our final announcements and then we had to join the network for our 8:30 NBC program. Dr. Lake was running long and we anticipated a problem, but he then skipped about 4 pages of his remarks without missing a beat and concluded on time. His supporters were going wild ... and little did anyone know what impact the program had among viewers. Dr. Lake had contributions mailed from surrounding areas, people gave him money when he made personal appearances the next day and his stock rose higher than could be expected.

Due to the response, we recorded another rally in Lumberton and a third rally was taped in New Bern by WNCT-TV in Greenville. These were shown around the state and Dr. Lake became a strong force in the gubernatorial primary. He eventually was defeated by Terry Sanford who became governor. The rallies were the talk of political circles for some time. It was another first for WECT.

Televising election returns was a complicated proceedure. The numbers were hand written as they were phoned in and then slid into appropriate slots on the boards. When the numbers came in rapidly the announcers worked hard to keep up; when they came in slowly, they had to think of something to say to fill with. Ballots were hand counted by precincts so the telecast sometimes lasted far into the night.

WECT always tried to produce programming that involved local residents.Here, in the early 60s, our version of American Band Stand

When the Jaycees sponsored the Soap Box Derby in 1969, WECT televised the event with George Deaton (holding mike) acting as the emcee

SPORTS

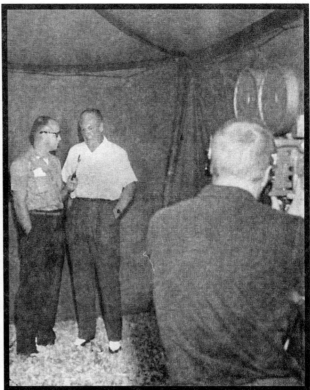

Wayne could always get prominent sports figures on camera. Here, on left, he talks with Baseball Hall of Famer Joe DiMaggio; on right , he interviews football great Red Grange during the Southern 500 at Darlington.

Sports has always been a big part of television and this area has always had a rich heritage of teams, individuals and events. To name just a few.... a PGA tournament had been played for several years at Cape Fear Country Club with the top professional golfers coming to Wilmington, Sonny Jurgensen had launched a great football career at Duke, Roman Gabriel was leading New Hanover High School football, Sam Bowens was not far from playing major league baseball and we would have Meadowlark Lemon playing with the Harlem Globetrotters. Dr. Hubert Eaton was aiding the education and tennis success of Althea Gibson. Athletic teams at New Hanover and Williston were among the best in the state and Wilmington College was beginning to be a force in junior college sports.

The 1957 NCAA basketball tournament was one of the turning points in college basketball in the state and on television. The Tar Heels made it to the Final Four and the games were televised. C.D. Chesley provided the telecasts to us and the response was beyond anything we could have imagined. First a three overtime win over Michigan State and another overtime win over Kansas and Wilt Chamberlin in the championship game. Bob West had been in the studio doing commercials during timeouts and when the camera went on him at the end of the Kansas game, Bob could only look into the camera and say' "we're number one". His smile said it all.

Our salesmen had some of our usual sponsors of commercials, but this event brought out Tar

Heel boosters clubs, the Atlantic Coastline Employees Service Club and just people on the street. This was the real start of televising college basketball. C.D. Chesley had started a venture that grew bigger and faster than anyone had imagined. In the beginning only one college game would be televised at night during the week, and it was so heavily watched that it hurt attendance at any other sports event scheduled for that night.

It became routine for us to contact Bill Brooks, athletic director and coach at Wilmington College, as soon as we received the television schedule. If he had any game on his calendar that was to be played on the same night as a tv game, Bill would call the other school and see if they couldn't switch their game to another night. Pembroke State also called for the TV schedule to compare with their home slate.

1960 - We televise our first local basketball game... Wilmington College vs Campbell College. Anncr. Wayne Jackson, cameraman Buck O'Shields, Eng. Ed Herring

In 1960 we got into the sports telecasting on a local level by taping a J.C. championship game between Wilmington and Campbell College at Brogden Hall which was the home court for Wilmington in those years. Campbell won the game which ended with a furious fight as Campbell tried to cut the nets. Our cameras stayed on the fight and when the tape was played later that night the viewers caught all the action.

Coach Brooks was not only athletic director and basketball coach, but baseball coach and his baseball teams won national J.C. baseball titles in 1961 and 1963, and finished second in 1962. We were happy to be one of the sponsors of a banquet for the national champs.

In the late 60s we decided to televise some high school football games on Friday night for playback Saturday morning. We focused on natural rivalries ...Wallace vs Burgaw, Whiteville vs Tabor City, Myrtle Beach vs Conway, Lumberton vs Elizabethtown and New Hanover vs Raleigh.

The sales department was able to sell the games in short order and the audiences, especially in the areas of the teams being shown, were very substantial.

We had never tried to do football telecasts but our engineering and production people did wonderful jobs getting everything right. And the coaches were very cooperative in giving us information as to any special plays or formations they might use in the game. They trusted us to keep it a secret.

Jack Holley, coaching at Tabor City, told me about his first three plays to be used against Whiteville... the quarterback faking a pitchout, then pitching out on the second play and throwing a pass on the third play. We told our producer to keep one of our two cameras on the quarterback and on the first play he rolled out, kept the ball, got two or three good blocks and went about 65 yards for a touchdown. Our camera was in close on him all the way and for that one play at least we looked like real network veterans.

The 1970 American Legion Post 10 baseball team made it to the Legion World Series in Klamath Falls, Oregon, and reporting on their success made the nightly sports shows top stories.

With no professional sports , fewer college sports and many fewer high schools, it was much easier to cover the action for our sports shows and we developed a close bond with the high school coaches. Leon Brogden, Jap Davis, Buck & Bill Hardee, Spike Corbin, Glenn Sasser, Joe Miller, Ray Durham and all others were always available if we needed them.

And being able to interview people like Gary Player, Jackie Robinson, Joe Louis, as well as our local athletes who went on to national and international fame made our local sports shows here in Wilmington seem special ... especially when the daily paper virtually ignored the black community.

Interviewing former boxing champ Joe Louis

In the late 50s we ventured into a sports feature that became a huge success and attracted pro football fans from all over the area. We partnered with the Atlantic Coastline R.R. and Amoco dealers to sponsor train trips to Washington to watch the Redskins in NFL games. The Redskins were on regional television and were the pro games we showed on Sunday afternoons. The Skins were our NFL team!

The first year of the special train we had about 250 people ... then it grew-and in 1960 some 800 people joined in the fun. The train left Wilmington at 5:00am on Sunday, stopped in Wallace, Warsaw, Goldsboro, Wilson and Rocky Mount and arrived in Washington at 12:25. We boarded buses to the game and after the game the buses took us back to the train and the trip ended in Wilmington at 12:35am.

Total price for the whole trip, including tickets to the game was $23.00 from Wilmington and $21.00 from Wallace. The Redskins game program said it was the largest family football party in history. They devoted three paragraphs in the program to our group. The party ended a year or two later when the Redskins changed their rules of dealing with special groups and the railroad could not go along with the new regulations. It was fun while it lasted.

1959- Wayne Jackson presents an NFL football to Community Boys Club member Ronnie Bell, on behalf of WECT and the Washington Redskins, as Club Executive Director Walter Bess looks on.

Through the years more and more college basketball became available to the viewer. The ACC was careful to not schedule telecasts on the nights when high schools traditionally played their games.

Camp Lejeune was the site of two of our biggest sports telecasts. In 1966 we taped the All-Marine Boxing Championships at Camp Lejeune and after playing the tapes on the station, we presented the program to the Marine Commandant for showing anywhere in the world, mainly for the men and women serving our country. One of those boxers was heavyweight Ken Norton, who later became a world champ and his son was a linebacker later in the NFL.

Then in 1968 we returned to Camp Lejeune and videotaped the Interservice Boxing Championships, featuring the men from the Army, Navy, Air Force and Marines. The 11 championship bouts were recorded August 15, and shown to our viewers August 17. The tapes were then sent to Armed Forces Radio and Television for showing to our troops around the world. Richard Williams handled the announcing for television. I had the enjoyable chore of doing live radio broadcast with Marine Master Gunnery Sergeant Kinsman.

This broadcast went to our troops on AFR around the world. It was my first and only chance to broadcast boxing on radio and I found out in a few seconds that you could not possibly describe every punch and all the action. I was out of breath after the first round and quickly altered my style. We received thanks from military leaders down to privates, all of whom enjoyed our efforts. This telecast stands out as one of our best efforts during my years at WMFD-WECT. Our engineering and production people did a superb job.

In 1964 and 1965 we did live telecasts of a Little League baseball tournament games. The 1964 game was the championship game of the North Carolina State Little Tar Heel League tournament, played at Optimist Park. As we did not have a surplus of equipment, we recorded the 6:00 news block so the cameras etc. could be taken to the park and be put in place for our telecast. We found that baseball is extremely difficult to cover as you never know where the ball will go once it is pitched. We only had two cameras and it was a difficult assignment but then again we were covering local activities and presenting something our viewers had not seen before on their TV screens ... local young boys competing in baseball.

The 1965 game was for the championship of the Wilmington City Optimist Little League tournament. The teams playing represented Leland and the Communications Workers (CWA). Many years later a gentleman in Lumberton told me he had pitched for Leland and would always remember the game and that he had been seen on TV.

To put it all together .... the sports world was busy .... never a dull moment.

EDITORIALS

In 1965 WECT ventured into the world of editorials and this continued into the 70s. The editorials were the responsibility of WECT and were subject to rebuttal ... and many of our opinions were answered by someone disagreeing with our thoughts. Some of the subjects were brought forth by Dan Cameron, WECT president, and some came from my mind ... but all were approved by Mr. Cameron before being aired. The final script was given an okay and were initialed by Mr. Cameron ...I still have one or two of those editorials with his initials on them. We would make announcements that equal time would be available to reply to the editorial. There could be only one reply ... if several viewers wanted to get equal time they would meet and select a spokesperson.

Sometimes, just when you think you are doing something good, a viewer can knock you down a peg or two. I still have a copy of a letter to the editor of the Star News from a lady in Currie. She had a few words about our regular programming, then wrote this.... "We can do without the many editorials by Mr. Wayne Jackson. I suggest he make 30 or 60 minute tapes of them and while he is on, we can switch to another channel and enjoy a good program."

Our subjects covered the many aspects of life and activities of the area .... roads, bond issues, government bodies and individual elected or appointed officials, desegregation of the schools, preservation of Ft. Fisher as an historic site, a container crane controversy at the State Port and the power of women.

In urging women to get more involved in government and elected officials, I stepped a bit to far and heard about it vociferously. The editorial ended with these words..."We're all for these women and all men should be too. If nothing else, at least as long as they spend their energy fighting the government, they'll leave their husbands alone". Boy, did I get phone calls from wives!

We received verbal feedback, but no requests for equal time when we advocated that someone from the black community be appointed to fill a vacancy on city council. As Mr. Cameron had been mayor of Wilmington in the early 5Os, he was well aware of the many problems facing the community and how the council makeup could solve many of those problems. In the late 70s we urged the appointment of Luther Jordan to city council. This was done and started Mr. Jordan on a long career, ending as a senator in the state legislature.

The days of station editorials seem to have come to an end. There are individual commentaries voiced, but nothing that carries station responsibility with it. The demise of local ownership may have much to do with the passing of editorials.

REMOTES & SPECIAL PROGRAMS

Your memory can fade somewhat when looking back over 50 years to try and remember just what was done and when. Let me take you back to the stations early years and recount some of the special programs we brought to the viewers. This will not be in any special order. Already mentioned have been sports, political and Azalea Festival telecasts.

In 1959 a program titled "You, Wilmington and Tomorrow", our station President, Dan Cameron, was featured to speak about the future of Wilmington and a better tomorrow. As a former mayor and local businessman he had vast insight into the years ahead. The program was instigated by the announcement that the Atlantic Coast Line Railroad was moving its headquarters and many hundreds of employees from Wilmington to Jacksonville, Florida. As all these people worked downtown, the news was devastating to the stores in Wilmington. This program came on at 8:30pm, preempting the scheduled network program. Mr. Cameron was a leader in forming the Committee of 100, a group that went looking for new business to replace the ACL. Through the years this group worked to bring in companies such as DuPont, G.E. & Corning among others.

A number of commercial businesses bought time for special programs. Cooperative Savings & Loan sponsored a one hour Christmas show put on videotape at the main lobby of their downtown office ... recorded on a Sunday in early December for playback Dec. 23. Featured on the program were the Williston High School choir and the Hanover Singers from New Hanover High School. There were no commercials during the program, only two brief messages for the holidays from Mr. Fred Willetts, president of Cooperative Savings and Loan, and his son, Fred Willetts, jr.

In 1960, the N.C. Highway Commission held an all-day open public hearing at Thalian Hall to discuss a possible new bridge over the Cape Fear River. This was televised live ... the first time the highway people had ever been on live TV. It started in the morning, broke for lunch, and continued in the afternoon. I will always remember one man standing and proclaiming..."Thank goodness for the bright lights of television to bring this to our people". Another statement from a participant came to be true... "We'll have a man on the moon before we have a bridge over the river" A man was on the moon a few weeks before the bridge was opened.

Setting up to televise the opening of the long-awaited Cape Fear Memorial Bridge. We were proud of our new "Hi-Tech" mobile vehicle.

Our cameras showed the USSNC being towed up the river to its present berth in 1961 and then in 1963 the N.C. General Assembly met on the battleship and our cameras took in the first legislative telecast outside of Raleigh. WECT played another part in the history of the USSNC. We helped lead fund-raising in the state by aiding in the production of a special program that was produced in the WRAL studios in Raleigh and shown statewide by every station in N.C. Hugh Morton was the spearhead in this production which featured Gov. Sanford, Andy Griffith, David Brinkley, Dick Groat of the Pittsburgh Pirates & former Duke star and singer Jane Morgan.

1961-Channel Six was there when the Battleship North Carolina came home to Wilmington

A DAY NEVER TO BE FORGOTTEN

Two Jimmys on the WECT staff were instrumental in two different ventures that came together on a fateful day. Jimmy Craig, sales executive, originated the idea to bring the USS North Carolina to Wilmington and establish it as a memorial to the men and women of World War II. Jimmy Moore, art director, was a member of the Civil Air Patrol, and was instrumental in urging WECT to be a co-sponsor of an air show at the airport.

1961 - General Manager Claud O'Shields welcomes guests to the CAP-WECT Air Show. This was the ill-fated show that turned into a tragedy.

The first show was in 1958.... then in 1959 the USAF Thunderbirds performed, followed in 1960 by the Navy Blue Angels and the Thunderbirds returned in 1961. With great support by the military at Myrtle Beach AFB, Cherry Point MCAS and Seymour Johnson AFB, the air show grew to be one of the biggest and best in the country. Military and civilian aerial performances, static display, renowned test pilot Bob Hoover, all combined to make it a special day.

1960- The Navy's Blue Angels were in town for the CAP-WECT air show.

61

WECT President Dan Cameron suits up for a flight with the Blue Angels during the 1960 WECT-Civil Air Patrol Air Show

In 1961, CAP Friendship Day was Sunday, Sept. 24, just a week before the USS North Carolina was scheduled to be brought up the river to its berth across from downtown Wilmington.

The Golden Knight paratroopers from Fort Bragg were to jump that day from a support plane of the Thunderbirds. Three of our staff were invited to join them ... Jimmy Craig, photographer John McNeill and sales manager C.D. Martin. Jimmy Craig was eager to see the berth for the USSNC from the air, John McNeill was to get aerial photos of the berth and the Golden Knights and C.D. Martin was a station representative. Army photographer Bobby Turner was the last person to climb aboard and said.. "I'll see you in a few minutes". He wanted to update his photo file on the Golden Knights.

The plane taxied off in a few minutes and soon was roaring down the runway for takeoff. We were televising live that day and our cameras caught the plane leave the ground, start climbing and suddenly stall and crash to the ground, breaking apart and burst into flames. Air Force crash and rescue units got to the plane in minutes and rescue operations began. Three men, the co-pilot, crew chief and army photographer Bobby Turner died at the scene. Rescue crews rushed all on the plane to the hospital, at that time James Walker Memorial Hospital.

Being on live television, the word of the crash spread rapidly. The hospital got word that many seriously injured patients would be arriving, and doctors and nurses reported to the hospital immediately. Some had witnessed the accident on TV and left for the hospital at once. Dozens of people came forward as blood donors.

You never think something like this will happen, but when it does…you never forget it! But the strange thing is, none of us can remember what we said on the air immediately after the tragedy happened…or if we said anything at all.

Jimmy Craig and John McNeill suffered severe burns from the fire. Jimmy died three weeks later. John died seven weeks after the crash. C.D. suffered burns and severe damage to a leg and spent a long period in the hospital and recovery before being able to return to the station. The staff was heartbroken and the next week when the battleship came into Wilmington we could only think of Jimmy and John and what they were missing. John was a very close friend and left a wife and three young children. He had not yet reached his 30th birthday.

Our wonderful staff pulled together ... assignments were changed for sales and the art department, tears were shed and prayers were given for Jimmy, C.D. and John.

Several of the paratroopers came back to Wilmington and to the station after they were released from the hospital. Lee and I were invited up to the NCO club at Fort Bragg for a party some months later. Some of them were still wearing casts but their spirits were high. Two of them stayed in touch for a few years until they went overseas or left the service.

That was our last air show,

Changing Times

The days of school integration, the closing of Williston and the opening of Hoggard, the Wilmington 10, shootings, burnings and the bombing of the Wilmington Journal building all brought a sense of uncertainty to Wilmington. What was going to happen next?

We bumped into news people from the networks and big city newspapers every day for several weeks. The National Guard was pressed into service, curfews were established and we were in an era we had not been in before.

The news department met at least twice a day to compare notes and to see what we knew and what might be coming up in the next few hours, or days. Ken Murphy, Betty Perkins and others on the news staff faced the biggest news challenge of their career. They handled it well, kept the public informed and worked long, tedious hours to do it.

One evening we heard of a gathering at Hugh McRae park. I went to see what was going on and upon entering the park was stopped by two men who stepped out from the side of the road, each carrying a rifle. When I asked "What are you guys doing?" they said they were deer-hunting. After going on into the park and observing many people and trucks and more firearms, I left and went downtown. Soon thereafter law enforcement men went into the park and dispersed the crowd.

Golden Frinks of the Southern Christian Leadership Conference and Leroy Gibson of the Rights of White People (ROWP) gave entirely different views of the situation in Wilmington.

The two high schools ... New Hanover and Hoggard.. were having daily disturbances from students who just couldn't get along with each other. Sheriffs deputies were on duty at each school.

Looking for some way possibly help the situation and make the public more aware of students feelings, we proposed to do some special programs, if the Board of Education would agree. Our proposal was to go to each school ... arrange two interview areas out near the entrance to the schools and interview students and basically ask them..."what's going on at school? why can't you all get along? tell me." Then let the students talk…we would not edit the tape...it would go on the just as it was put on tape. Ken Murphy would talk with one student, then pass it on to me for another student. We went back and forth like this for an hour ... taking the students as   they came to us ... one at a time.

Both programs were then played back at night from 8:00 - 900 pm, preempting the scheduled network program. How much it helped I do not know, but students were heard and more people could understand their feelings.

When we had first presented the idea to the school board they looked at us like..."are you crazy? you want to do what?" But in the end they said "let's try it ... maybe it will help".

During that time Meadowlark Lemon, Wilmington native and star of the Harlem Globetrotters was in town and he came on the air one night for a live 30 minute program. Meadowlark urged calm and understanding in the community and a stop to any violence.

Slowly the violence and bitter feelings eased off and the community started to get along a little better but underneath it all resentment lingered. Those were very trying days, weeks and months.

TV Was Changing Too....

Those of us appearing in front of the camera wore no makeup. We went on camera just as we looked-for better or worse. It saved time and money. Besides, we were all young and handsome, weren't we? In any case, we made no attempt to hide any blemishes.

There were many parties ... in and out of the station. The sales department held several parties in various areas that we covered with our signal and programs. Advertisers and potential advertisers were invited for a few hours of food and fun. There were no sales pitches, just a few minutes to say thanks for coming and thanks for your business. The customers seemed to appreciate the relaxing evening and their relationship with the sales department. A number of these parties featured boiled shrimp and that made for a special evening.

There were a number of station parties for employees. Dan and Betty Cameron knew how to put together a great evening and our yearly Christmas parties were much anticipated. And we had mullet roasts in the yard outside the station on Shipyard Blvd. Dan got into his cooking clothes and led the way.

All of this, plus the fact that we were learning to do many things with little equipment led to stronger working arrangements between various departments. For our remote telecasts, engineering, production and the on-camera people all worked as a team, helping each other reach a common goal ... a successful program. Each department had its own functions and it required understanding to get everything right.

Claud O'Shields, general manager, and Clint Long, program director, were the early leaders in getting everyone to work as a team. They encouraged us all to come up with ideas to make a better presentation on the air, to have sales ideas, to make positive suggestions for news stories, suggest guests for interview programs... in short ... don't be hesitant or bashful, give us your ideas, help us become a better TV station.

When we celebrated our 10th anniversary, there were 41 people on the staff ... at least 10 of those have died ... nearly half of the 41 live in the Wilmington area. Some had moved away but came back to Wilmington. In 1974, at the 20th anniversary dinner, the staff had grown to 54.

```
** DAN D. CAMERON ................................................................. PRESIDENT & DIRECTOR
*  J. S. BRODY ............................................. VICE-PRES., ASSIST. SEC., & DIRECTOR
   PAUL A. BRISSETTE, JR .......................................... VICE-PRES., & GENERAL MANAGER
*  BRUCE B. CAMERON ............................................... SEC., TREAS., & DIRECTOR
   JABE V. HARDEE ...................................................... ASSIST. SECRETARY
*  LEO BRODY ................................................................................. DIRECTOR
```

JERRY BACKUS	BILL KIMBRELL
DIANE BARRY	MARY KING
DOLLIE BEATTY	* MIKE LOIZIDES
JUDY BENTLEY	** C. D. MARTIN
** NESTOR BORUCH	KEN MURPHY
TOMMY BOYD	BOB OWEN
CAROL BROCK	ETTA PATRICK
RONNIE BROTHERS	LES PATERNOTTE
MERVAIN BROWN	BETTY PERKINS
PAM BROWN	C. L. PERKINS
* JIM BURNS	ALICE RAYNOR
JOHN CALLUM	SAM RHAMES
DANNY CAMERON	* DOT ROMEO
DIXIE COLEMAN	ED SALES
* BILL ELKS	TED SAMPLEY
MAXINE FREEDMAN	JOE SCHLEGEL
ALAN FUSSELL	BARRY SIKES
* BOBBY GURGANIOUS	MARGARET SMITH
LATHAM HAMNER	CLIFF SNOW
AL HARDEE	TOM SWEENEY
BOB HARDESTY	BOBBY TOWNSEND
RONNIE HAWES	ED WARD
TOM HEAD	ALLENE WARREN
PAT HILLMAN	ERNIE WHITMEYER
* WAYNE JACKSON	KLEIST WIDEMAN
SUZANNE JEFFERSON	MARTHA WILLIAMS
BOBBY JORDAN	MIKE WYCKOFF

```
**   20 Years Continuous Service
*    10 or More Years Continuous Service
```

It is interesting to see where some of our people went after leaving the station. The Buie brothers, Ken & Don, went to General Electric and are now retired, Buck O'Shields, who had worked in production and sales, went into his own business and also was elected to the county commission for several terms, Two men in production went separate ways. Howard Morgan became a commercial airlines pilot and Jack Forehand managed a TV station in San Antonio, Texas. Roland Register worked in the film room as a young man and in later years became tax administrator for New Hanover County.

WILMINGTON, NORTH CAROLINA

In 1963 some lessons were learned when we had a contest to select a Pirate Girl to represent the station and to be the logo for our station identification slides. After being trapped off-stage by some irate mothers who thought their daughters were being unfairly judged, I swore never to have any part in any beauty contest ever again. Helen Wall of Myrtle Beach became our one and only Pirate Girl. We never had another one!

Those of us who appeared in front of the camera owe a great big thank you to those people in engineering and production who set up all the equipment and props and made the production possible. Without them nothing would get on the air.

Ed Herring was our first chief engineer, followed by Bill Elks, who came in 1957 when ownership changed. Bill had been at WNCT-TV in Greenville. These men were unflappable and accomplished near miracles with the equipment available in those early years. It was their work that made our program ideas become realities. Parades, political rallies, sports events, highway department hearings and other programs we have discussed were successful because of these men and their engineers ... men like Nestor Boruch, John Kondracki, Mike Loizides, Bob Owen, Cliff Snow and Latham Hamner to name a few, will never be forgotten for what they did. Whenever a program idea was put in front of them they almost always said, "yes, we can do that". Very seldom did they reject an idea as not doable.

To Ed and Bill ... and all the men in their department, I say "well done". It was a pleasure to work with you.

Two ladies deserve special mention. I will never forget Bobbie Marcroft, who wrote copy for commercials and other announcements and was a guiding light to people in the station.

A great mind and a great inspiration to everyone, Bobbie had a sharp wit and was full of ideas to help us all do our jobs. Bobbie died in 2003, but she lives on in our minds.

And Dorothy Romeo, who personifies the word "family". Dot was sales secretary and kept a book with the birth dates and anniversary dates of many, many people. After all these years cards are still received from Dot as those two dates come around.

As I look back, I am happy to have chosen WMFD-WECT as a career and am proud of all the things the station accomplished over the years. We were pioneers and paved the way for the people who followed us. We had a family ... we were close to each other ... and still are. Mr. Dunlea and Mr. Cameron were men who guided us through the years, encouraged us and backed us through both the good and lean years.

And I still get a good feeling when people come up and say... "I grew up watching you on TV when I was a little boy (or girl)." It's nice to know they remember.

Now it's time to sign off.

Yes!

CBS JOINS
WMFD-TV

And Regular Programs

With Live Daytime
TELEVISION

BEGINNING AT 11:00 A. M.

October 1st

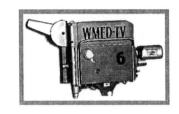

TV and Politics... A Brave New Approach
John Jay Burney III
Attorney, former District Attorney, former State Senator

I remember my first experience with WMFD-TV. It was early on, in April of 1954, right after they went on the air. I was District Solicitor then, and they invited me and Judge Clifton Moore to be on television...I don't remember exactly why or what we were supposed to talk about.

Anyhow, I used my first television opportunity to congratulate the Boys Home of Lake Wacammaw, which had just opened. Then I went out and bought a television set for $50 from Todd Furniture...it was a big bulky thing, black and white of course ...and watched the first movie that Channel Six ever aired. It was "GI Joe', the story of war correspondent Ernie Pyle.

The people of Wilmington were real excited when television came to town. Back then, everybody knew everybody....they even knew their dogs... and of course they knew a lot of the people who were on the air, so that made television a big event.

In 1960 we put on the first "live" political rally in the whole country. Dr. I. Beverly Lake, who had taught me in law school, was running for Governor and he called me up and asked me what I could do to help him. I called Dan Cameron and asked him if we could do a live rally from the Court House and he said "I don't know. I don't think anybody has ever done that before."

According to Wayne Jackson, that was to be one of the first "remotes" that the station had done, and although he called every TV station then on the air in North Caroline to ask for advice, no one could help because none of them had ever attempted a live political rally before. Nobody knew exactly how to go about doing it.

But in spite of that, Mr. Cameron called me back a little later and said WECT was willing to try it if we were.

We got people in here from all the surrounding counties who were interested in Dr. Lake, and we packed the courthouse full. Nobody will ever believe this, but when we went on the air that night, we had not rehearsed one iota. We hadn't planned anything...we just started.

I had gotten Col. McClellan, who had been my father's law partner and who was then my law partner, to introduce Dr. Lake, and when the cameras came on and they threw all those bright lights on him, he just froze! He couldn't say a word…and I know he had been doing public speaking for fifty years.

Anyhow, we finally got started and let me tell you, that thirty minutes just flew by. We wanted to keep going and I asked Dan Cameron if we could. He said, "John, I'd be glad to let you keep going if I could, but I don't know how to."

We had just been allotted that thirty minutes and then they had to join the network.

But let me tell you, that rally really got attention and money from people who wanted to support Dr. Lake's candidacy began to pour in.

We went on to do several other televised rallies in places like Lumberton and New Bern, but those were done on that brand new invention, video tape. That live rally in Wilmington was a national first.

In fact, we asked the stations in Asheville and Charlotte if we could come and put on a live rally with them, but they said they didn't need any of that "country hick" stuff.

Since Dr. Lake carried all the areas where we did televised rallies, I often wonder what the outcome would have been if we had been able to do it in those other places. Unfortunately, Dr. Lake lost his bid for governor.

Politics on television was really different on those days. Now, the commercials are like selling soap. You see somebody walking and somebody talking for thirty seconds, but you don't really get to know anything about them. Back then, like when I ran for the State Senate, we bought five minutes at a time, or sometimes even thirty minutes, and we went on the air and just told people what we thought and where we stood.

Television was a great medium then, in the fifties and sixties. It changed the face of politics. When candidates went on the air they didn't have all these sound effects and visuals effects and copy writers…they were just themselves and that's what people saw.

Television, a Brand New Teaching Tool
Ann Dunsford Mills
Hostess, children's programming and many other duties
1954 - 1962

As I sit to write a few things about working at Channel Six, many things flood my memory. There are many funny and happy memories but also some times of sadness.

I go back in time to 1954 when I first was associated with WMFD Radio and Television. Just after I graduated from high school in the spring of 1954 I was given the opportunity to do a fifteen minute television program, "Saturday Sunday School". Children from area churches would come to the studio on Princess Street, around 5:30 p.m. on a Saturday afternoon, and participate in an on-the-air Sunday School on Saturday.

Ann Dunsford was just out of high school when she began hosting a series of children's programs. Ann had a special knack for communicating with youngsters

The format was simple… we would sing songs and I would tell a Bible Story. At that time the station had one camera and an overhead microphone. I guess I was to young to be afraid of anything, possibly not even realizing how many people were at home watching. We played it by ear as there were no TelePrompters, only a few notes that hung on the camera. If the camera was too far away, forget the notes. On the other hand, sometimes the cameraman would bring that huge camera so close that my eyes felt like they were crossing and I couldn't see any cue cards at all. They thought it was really funny!

So, most things were memorized and if you got it wrong it just went out over the air anyway.

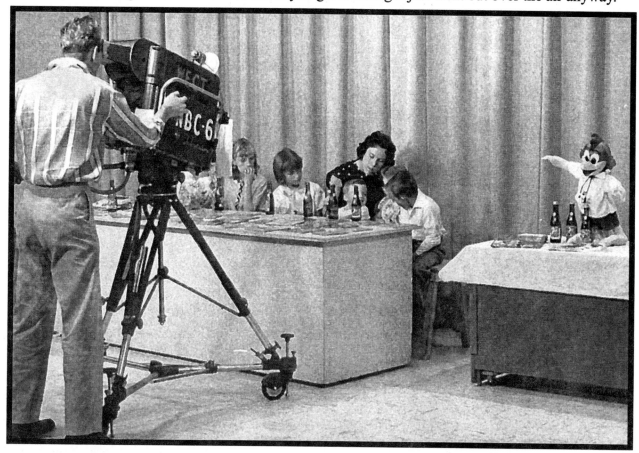

You never knew what kids would do, so the cameraman had to be alert

"Saturday Sunday School" went on for a couple of years and during that time I started working as a receptionist, weekdays and on Saturday. People who worked in television then had to be adaptable, to say the least.

When you worked at the station on Princess Street you did not need to be a member of a gym, even if there had been such a thing way back then. We had our own gym called " stairs". The radio station and offices were on the second floor and television studio on the third floor, with no elevator and so we walked up and down those stairs many times a day. It amazes me, thinking back, how large items for advertising and other purposes were carried to the third floor.

The stairs at the station went along with creaking floors and all the other things that were in an old building. There was a store on the ground floor and this was only one of many stores and offices up and down Princess Street. We knew most of the people on the street and always had a good time passing the time of day with them. I remember we used to get lunch, dinner, or just a cup of coffee in a diner around the corner on Third Street. I wish I could remember the names of all the stores and people but that was a long time ago.

Memories are wonderful, especially the good times. One such memory is working with Dot Romeo in traffic. We had a great time and right now it doesn't seem like hard work, although I know that at the time we thought differently. I remember at one time Dot was twice my age. I think I may have been twenty-one and she was forty-two. During all these years I don't remember either of us forgetting each others birthday. I keep reminding her that she is twice my age and she sure looks good.

During the time working in traffic (which, to the uninitiated, is the exacting keeping of logs of every second of air time, what's on when…and with who) I started doing "Kiddie Time" and also some commercials. Again, versatility was the key word! After Katie Godwin left, I took her place as "Skipper Ann" and my boat was the "Chug Tug". As you can tell, programming for young children was a very important part of our agenda. Its also one of the most interesting and demanding because…you never know what a child's going to say!

Again no TelePrompters and only one camera. Later on we did get another camera and eventually that hi-tech magic, color. As with "Saturday Sunday School" children would come to the studio from all over the viewing area. On "Kiddie Time" we would sing, march, do exercises, have story time and a lot of other activities. No animated cartoons, no special effects…but the kids loved it.

George Tregembo would come each week from the Tote-Em-In Zoo and bring animals. These were especially good times for the children. I met many children during these times and the memories are wonderful. Take a careful look at the photos with this story…you may be in them!

Ann hosted a special occasion featuring the offspring of staff members. Can you believe they are all middle-aged people now?

Sometimes, even now, an older adult will come up to me and say that they were on "Saturday Sunday School" or "Kiddie Time". Boy does that make me feel old!

Thinking about the animals on "Kiddie Time" made me remember a time at the station, downtown, when someone brought a huge snake to a program and it took about five or six of us to hold it. The one thing we lacked was a cameraman, as he had locked the camera and hurriedly left the studio.

We celebrated all of the holidays, whether religious or secular, and these were very special programs for the children taking part. One year at Halloween we were bobbing for apples during the program. I was showing the children how it should be done and the next thing I knew my head was under water. The cameraman, Frank Piner, decided that I needed to go all the way to the bottom of the bucket for an apple. Needless to say this went over really big with the children as well as the studio crew. I was dripping wet, down to my shoulders, but we kept on going. The studio crew were always up to something and it sure made life interesting and a lot of fun.

I was at Channel Six from late 1954 until 1962. This was a very important part of my life. I met and married my husband, Dallas, who was a cameraman at the time. One of my sons was born while we were working at the station and I left just before the birth of my second son. I must not leave out that after I left we also had two daughters.

Jackie Pastis, Ann Dunsford Mills, Bebe Bryant and Helen Romeo pose with visiting TV actor Ty Hardin, star of the western series "The Outlaw"

Along with the happy times there were some very sad times. The loss of Frank Piner, John McNeil and Jimmy Craig was a very sad time for those of us who were working or had worked at the station. I often remember Frank, John, and Jimmy and they will always be a wonderful part of my life.

Life has gone on for those of us in the early days of television. Many of us went on to other careers but to have been there at the very beginning of television in our area was an experience that will always be with me. Thank you Mr. Dick Dunlea, WMFD, who is no longer with us and Mr. Cameron, WECT, for allowing me to have a little part of the beginning of such a great industry.

People who were on Channel Six quickly became local celebrities. Here, Ann Dunsford Mills and Bill Weathers greet their fans during one of the first televised Azalea Festival parades

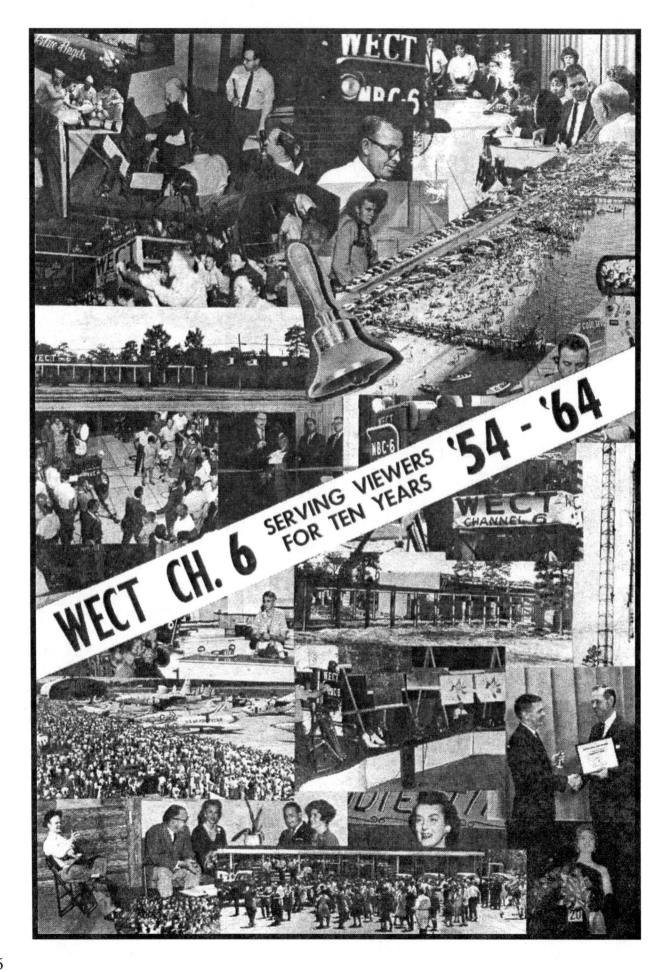

WECT CH. 6 SERVING VIEWERS FOR TEN YEARS '54 - '64

Television and Children …
A Winning Combination
Katherine Godwin

In 1954 there was much local excitement at the news that our very own television station was coming to Wilmington!

At first, WMFD-TV aired only a few hours a day with only local news, sports, local weather, and Western Theater. At first we had no network programming due to the FCC regulations-so many hours had to be aired before network availability.

We gathered around this wonderfully new medium each evening with great anticipation.

A few months later, my husband, Bill and our three year old son Johnny were off to visit my uncle's home in Virginia for a short vacation. There, TV was not new at all. Each morning a special program came on for young children and Johnny sat glued to the TV. He enjoyed the show so much that he really didn't want to leave and come home. I was so carried away with his reaction that I couldn't get it out of my mind.

But on our local station there was nothing especially for the little ones, so after returning home I mustered up enough courage to go to the local station on Princess St., in downtown Wilmington , to ask if there were any plans in the near future for a children's show.

Mr. R.A. Dunlea, station owner and manager said "No, not at this time. Are you interested in doing such a show?" Well, I must say I choked up, but after thinking of the experience with Johnny in Virginia I said "Yes, I am!"

Mr. Dunlea informed me that a guy from Illinois was coming here to be program director—the guy was Wayne Jackson ! Wayne asked me to plan a show and present it to him and others on staff. I did and they liked it and that was the beginning of WMFD-TV's KIDDIE TIME, with hostess Katy (Katherine Godwin).

Wayne gave me the name "Katy", and until this day, that's what all of the TV folks call me. At first the show was on 30 min. three times a week and later 30 min. each afternoon and finally, an hour show each afternoon, when we added some cartoon films.

In the photo handwriting: WMFD-TV, NBC-6 Television, KT, CHUG TUG, "Skipper" Katy Chug-Tug Boat, Honey Bunny (Annell Mohr), Katherine Godwin

***Honey Bunny (Annell Kirkland) and Skipper Katy talk with young guests
aboard the CHUG TUG BOAT***

Working in TV was quite a challenge . I had worked with children at church and 4-H Clubs, but never any experience in TV, especially live TV! With live TV what you do is what they see…no editing out errors !

But somehow, each day things would fall into place. The show began with a nursery rhyme theme. Later, I changed the format to a nautical theme in the CHUG TUG BOAT. Children from all over Wilmington and surrounding areas would be on the show. We recognized birthdays, visited TV land with the MAGIC MIRROR and had games and relays.

One day I saw a elderly man outside the studio who said that there were some things that he didn't particularly like on the show. I simply replied that it was a children's show, not for adults, and he walked away shaking his head. Some people still didn't realize that TV was for children too.

We had stories and art lessons and music. Lucille Horrell Shepard played the piano each day. Later in the show we added a side-kick known as HONEY BUNNY, —Annell Mohr Kirkland -was the first. This led to the Bunny Hop as a special feature.

I got to meet so many wonderful children. One day as I was walking down Front St. , a precious little girl ran up to me so very excited, with her eyes so big, and asked, " Miss Katy, how did you get out of my TV set ?" There was one little cute red-headed girl that came on the show several time . Some afternoons I would have riddle time. Some cute riddles would be asked and the kids would get a big laugh. One day this cute little girl said, "I have a riddle," —— so I said O.K. Well the riddle she told would make your face turn red ! (remember we were on live!).

But I guess I didn't learn my lesson, because a few weeks later she was on the show again and asked to tell another riddle. I really didn't think this would happen again but ... it did! After the show was over I cornered her outside and asked her where she had heard these riddles, and she said, "My dad, and he told me to tell them." Needless to say, I didn't let her tell any more riddles.

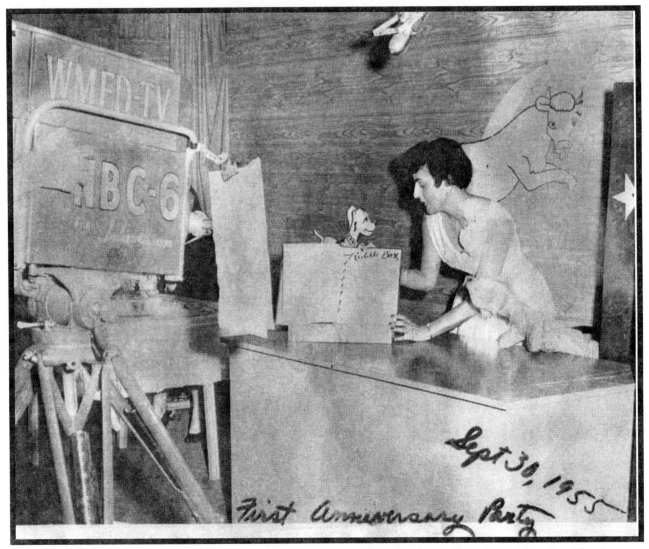

It was a special day when we celebrated the program's first birthday in 1955

I had an impressive list of sponsors of the show .... there was the Camera Shop with the precious Ginger Dolls, Tru-Ade Orange, Sundrop, Wanet's Sausage, Golding's, Efirds, J.C. Penny and many others!

A dog food company from Durham wanted to present a commercial. One problem; they wanted me to eat some of the dog food on the show to prove that is was pure & clean! Well, can't you just see some of these little ones eating with Fido and saying, "It's O.K., Miss Katy eats it on TV"

Music, reading stories, and laughing a lot were what made the show fun

Along with the Kiddie Show, I also had the opportunity to be on Wayne's show, "Relax With Jax" in the afternoon. I'd put on a different hat, assume a different character, and help with interviews. I can remember being Kingfish, Sunshine Sue, Kathryn Grayson, and Arnold Palmer, and many others. Wayne did a great show! I enjoyed working with him.

Also, I had the opportunity to do many commercials ..... one of my favorites was Nesbitts Dress Shop. I loved wearing all those beautiful outfits. I really didn't make much money because I wanted to purchase everything that I modeled !

There was a weekly night show, sponsored by the Wilmington Gas Co. All of the commercials were live and I had to go down to the station for a one minute commercial in the middle of the program . One night, the show was a murder mystery ... a man was trying to murder his wife using their gas stove ...and in the midst of this grisly scene I had to pop-up and do a commercial for the Gas Company. Not exactly the best placement for that spot!

I remember one experience that was so scary ! I had a sitter with Johnny each afternoon. On Mondays, the sitter would take him to our church for the Sunbeam Meeting. About halfway through the show that afternoon, someone rushed in from the control room and held up a sign that said I had an emergency phone call. I asked Lucille to play a game with the children while I rushed to the phone. A voice on the other end said "Your little boy has been run over and killed! ......and then they hung up.

I frantically called the church and asked the secretary to check on Johnny .... she did and returned to say that "He's having a great time in the Sunbeam meeting." I was trembling and pale white but returned to the show like nothing had happened. I knew that there was someone out there waiting to see my reaction and I did not want to give them the pleasure of seeing me fall apart ! Talk about "the show must go on"!

I left the show for a while due to Johnny being in school ... he was gone in the mornings, and I was gone in afternoons and I really didn't have much time with him. I continued to do commercials and a few other things.

When the station, now with the call letters WECT-TV, moved to the new location on Shipyard Blvd, I was asked to do another children's show. By that time I had had another precious little son, Terry, who was a toddler, so I was hesitant. My sister encouraged me to do the new show and she volunteered to take care of the boys.

I called the new show "KATY'S CABIN", added some new & different features, and did the show until the station discontinued doing local shows and went to the national network children's shows.

These were very special years and I thank God for the opportunity of offering children a fun-filled, clean program created specially for them.

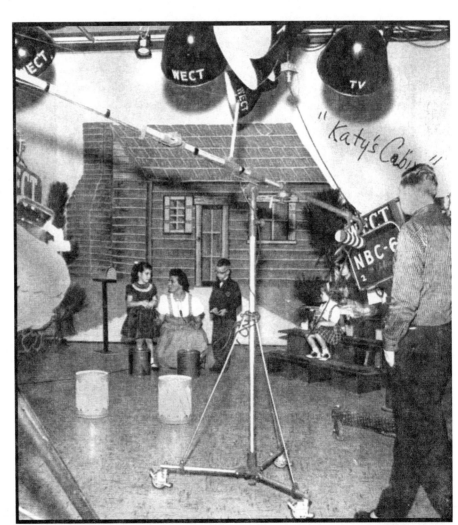

Katy created her second show, "Katy's Cabin", which gave local children another chance to be part of a live TV show

But although my years as a full-time television person were over, I just couldn't entirely let it go, so I worked at WMFD-TV and WECT-TV off and on during the 50's, 60's, & 70's as a "on the air" personality. It was a wonderful and exciting part of my life.

In the Fifties and early Sixties commercials were done live. Here, Katy Godwin was being careful not to spill that Sundrop she was pouring. If a mishap did occur on the air, a "make good" commercial was done free of charge.

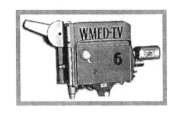

Present at the Creation...
A Backward Glance
Bill Rogers

Sometime between the end of World War II and the mid-1950's television stations blinked on all across America, ushering in the true beginning of the modern age and the world's most powerful communication medium that fundamentally changed the world and its people forever!

Television would, in time, change the way people lived, thought and acted about every facet of human endeavor. It created a much smaller world in terms of the speed at which news events and other information traveled instantaneously to and from every corner of the world through the use of space satellites.

Television was aborning!!

Smile, we're on LIVE CAMERA in living black and white. In those early years my fellow pioneers and I exhibited raw courage when we strolled in front of a television camera because we all found out that, sooner or later, anything could happen and usually did.

When all went according to the script there were smiles all 'round but when a monumental goof occurred there was no place to hide. We were left with our faces hanging out and we had to use whatever God-given resources we didn't know we had to get out of the mess. We might look for assistance from the control room, the cameraman, the boom mike man, the janitor - but, my friend, there was no help there - it was live camera only, pardner - and uh, lots a luck fellow pioneer!!!

Bob West was our first and only newscaster; in fact he was our total news department. He had at least one God-given gift - he had a phenomenal memory. He was able to present the evening news looking us straight in the eye and seldom looking down to check his copy. This made for a very believable and authoritative presentation. In my estimation, Bob was Mr. Television at Channel Six.

My confidence in Bob was just a tiny bit shaken one day when he and another on-air personality did a vacuum cleaner commercial for MacMillan and Cameron that they did several times a week. Bob held the Mac and Cam Cleaner and the other guy held brand X. The idea was that Bob was to demonstrate the power of the Mac and Cam Cleaner by taking a ping-pong ball away from brand X. It was working like a charm until during one presentation the Mac and Cam Cleaner evidently wasn't feeling very well and the brand X cleaner took the ball away from the Mac and Cam unit.

Pure consternation spread over Bob's face and riotous laughter erupted from the Control Room. Bob, ole buddy, you couldn't run and you couldn't hide, could ya! I understood! ! !

I wonder whatever happened to Jesse James (Jay Bird) Merritt? Now, there was a fellow who burned a two-ended candle at all four ends! He stood at about 5 feet 4 inches tall with a permanent grin spread across his face. There didn't seem to be anything he hadn't done, wasn't doing, or wasn't planning to do. Jay Bird was completely irrepressible…and probably the best cameraman I ever saw.

Many times I saw him push the camera to get a running start, jump on the tripod and coast right up to the on-air person, creating a zoom-in visual effect. Now, this didn't work perfectly every time and the camera didn't have brakes and occasionally the on-air person would have to be checked for bruises and abrasions.

Channel Six aired a half-hour wild animal program featuring all kinds of wildlife which could be seen by the visiting public every day of the week at the Tote-Em-In-Zoo located at Monkey Junction on Carolina Beach Road. The television program was called "Safari" and featured the zoo's curator, George Tregembo and yours truly as host. One particular evening George was featuring reptiles. We were all in our assigned places on camera. Chet Rogers was our floor manager and Jay Bird was our ace one-cameraman.

About fifteen minutes into the program - I don't know exactly what happened but George Tregembo lost his grip on a large rattlesnake and when the snake got loose on the floor all H—broke loose!!! I climbed atop the display table, Chet was looking for anything to climb on to get him to higher ground.

George Tregembo, with his snake grabber, was hunting in the dark for the snake and Jay Bird was nowhere to be found. We later found out that Jay Bird had abandoned the camera in great haste and had reached Princess Street, three stories below, in 51/2 seconds. This record has never been broken! Folks, I honestly don't remember what happened after that. I do know that it was pure bedlam there for a while until George got the rattler back in the box. I could also hear gales of laughter coming from the control room!! I can truly say that that evening there was no place to hide!!!

The first time I ever saw Johnny Thomas I was sitting in my living room at Riverside Apartments. It was the Saturday afternoon before reporting to Channel Six the following Monday for my first day at the station. I turned on the TV and there was Johnny at the piano accompanying a small fellow sitting on a stool singing "My Funny Valentine." I found out later his name was Herbie Barnes.

Announcing was his job, but Bill could belt out a tune when a singer was needed

Johnny Thomas was one of the nicest and friendliest persons I ever met. He always had a smile for everyone and he was so very talented. I guess that if the station needed a fair haired boy it would have been him. I mean this in the finest kind of way! He was so kind, in fact, that he agreed to back me up on the piano two evenings a week after the evening news as I sang two or three songs. Believe me I needed some strong backing!!!

Johnny wasn't much more than a teenager, handsome and blessed with musical talent - and, well-you know, I guess he broke a lot of young girls hearts along the way. What a terrible burden to bear!!!

MAN IN THE MIDDLE

Wayne Jackson had no natural enemies. He always had a smile on his face. Wayne was a guy who had the ability to understand both sides of our television business: the owner-management side and the talent-technical side. He was the glue that held us all together through all our foibles - most of our foibles!

Wayne was always seeking ways to make our on-air product better. He met with us regularly in critique sessions in which we all discussed ways we could improve our on-air work. Any personal criticism was done in private and in the kindest sort of way.

I feel quite certain that Wayne had his share of ups and downs during his long tenure at Channel Six - thirty-plus years!! He held many important positions along the way including weather, news and sports casts, special program work, program director and station manager.

He spent his entire television career at one station - Channel Six. Wayne, you were one of our favorite television pioneers and all of us hold you highest esteem!!! A Pioneer of both Radio and Television

I don't remember the first time I met Mr. R. A. Dunlea, Sr. He sort of drifted into my consciousness because I didn't hang around the corporate offices as a habit.

I do remember that on one occasion Mr. Dunlea was telling two or three of us about a radio announcer he once employed who had a marvelous voice but, he said, as the day progressed the announcer's words became more and more slurred. Mr. Dunlea said he looked everywhere - in drawers, behind desks and on ledges, trying to find a bottle. He said he finally lifted the commode tank lid in the men's bathroom and found it tied to the flusher handle.

Mr. Dunlea pioneered radio in Wilmington in the 1930's and 1940's and then… in the mid 1950's… here comes television!!! I can only imagine how he faced the possibility of putting a million-dollar television station on the air and hiring all the people it would require to keep it there.

Sometime, early on in the 1950's Mr. Dunlea, Sr. and Jr. teamed up with Mr. Dan Cameron in order to share the financial burden and project the television operations into the future.

THE GIRLS AT CHANNEL SIX

Katherine Godwin combined beauty and talent in so many of her on-air responsibilities. Katy told me during our August 2002 meeting that she sat on the panel that auditioned me when I came to work for the station in the mid-50's. I asked her how I did and she replied: "You were hired, weren't you?" She was one of the bright personalities in our television operation.

Ann Dunsford Mills was another of the fine young women who worked on the air at Channel Six during those wonderful years in the 1950's. Ann made a name for herself as the hostess of a religious program for children on Saturday afternoon entitled "Saturday Sunday School."

Jane Rhett hosted a cooking show a couple of days a week during the middle of the day. I remember we all looked forward to eating the delightful results of her culinary presentations when her program ended.

Jackie Pastis Margoles — our own Greek Goddess! Jackie was tall, beautiful and talented!! She anchored one of the first early morning newscasts at Channel Six. Eventually she moved on to Washington, D.C. where she remained involved in television news. There was never a dull moment when Jackie was around.. in fact, some of her escapades were legendary around the station.

Betty Hutson Perkins was and is a superb reporter-writer. She became our first female reporter to take camera in hand and go out to cover the fields of crime and violence. In the late 60's, she and Ken Murphy WERE the news department. of. Presently she is busy compiling and editing this book so that all these memories can be kept.

OTHER PEOPLE I REMEMBER

Howard Morgan was on the technical staff at WMFD-TV in the mid-50's. Howard was always so warm and friendly. He went to my hometown of Clarkton, N.C. and installed the first television set my parents ever had. Howard always had flying in his blood. He would fly anyway and anywhere he got the opportunity. Howard went on to become a pilot for National Airlines and ended a long career as a Captain and Check Pilot for Pan American Airlines. We are very proud of Howard!

Roland Register was on the technical staff at Channel Six and went on to a career in New Hanover County government.

Jack Forehand was a technical staff member, progressed through the television industry in various parts of the country.

Chet Rogers, my first cousin, was involved in various aspects of Channel Six's studio operation. He went on to a fruitful career at Burlington Industries.

When television came to Wilmington in 1954 no one had the slightest inkling as to what it would become. For all we knew it would just be like radio with pictures —kind of like a big toy to play with. This didn't mean that we didn't take it all seriously. I don't think any of us could have imagined the powerful impact television has had on Wilmington, the state, the nation and the world. It has created enormous wealth in so many areas of our lives - industry, the arts and sports to name just a few.

It has affected our religious, moral and philosophical outlook on life. Many of the changes brought by this great medium are good and many are not so good. But there is one thing for sure - television is here to stay!!!

And now, for a few moments, I'd like to turn to the more personal and give you a glimpse of some of my thoughts and impressions of those early years in the television industry.

I began as a booth announcer, doing commercials and station breaks. I pulled time in front of the camera. In those days everyone did a little of everything. I kept the boom-mike properly placed for the on-air people and I even switched/directed programs from the control room.

I look at the local and national networks today and realize that they have more people in their news operations than we had in our entire staff.

Two dramatic innovations were the arrival of color and videotape. Suddenly we had to become conscious of the colors we wore on camera and everything shown on camera had to be color coordinated.

When videotape came along I think a great deal of the fun of television went out the window. Everything became very surgical and precise. No more mistakes went out over the air. (well, hardly ever). All commercials and many other programs were pre-recorded and from then on television broadcasting became deadly serious! This could almost be predicted because keeping a TV station on the air was becoming more and more expensive.

Putting all these innovations aside I believe the greatest asset a television station has is its people. Television was, is and will continue to be a people business. I've seen some unsavory characters in our industry who operated in their own self interest but the greatest majority of my fellow pioneers were just plain good and down-to-earth people who loved what they were doing and wanted television to be everything it could be for the greater benefit of the viewer.

Should I be asked for advice from a person thinking about a career in television I'd suggest he/she should work hard on their people skills, eliminate the egotistical and self-centered aspects of the personality and concentrate on what you can do to help the industry solve some of its problems. Be a good team player and don't forget one important truth - "nobody ever achieved anything worthwhile without the help of so many other good people."

Well, if we can stop the Hobby Horses I guess I'll get off. I enjoyed my association with all the pioneers at WECT. They helped me along the way in my personal development in television and in gaining some maturity and wisdom in my personal life.

Of all the towns and cities in which I worked in the television industry, Wilmington was my favorite. Every time I cross the Memorial Bridge I feel as if I'm coming home. Wilmington is truly my "Shining City on the Hill."

Thanks for piping me aboard, folks. It was a heck of a ride!!!

Early 60s...Dan Brinson explains the workings of the bulky new tape machine to a a a staff member. This equipment was a big step forward, adding new capabilities.

What a Way to Start a Career!

Lois "Twiddle" McConkey

Where do I begin? My beginning was "Over At Al's", a half-hour weekday program. If any of us involved in this new venture had really thought about what we were trying to do, we probably would not have done it!

But, it never occurred to us to be nervous, even though live TV was something none of us knew anything about. That's the confidence of youth and inexperience, I guess.

We had a wonderful group Over At Al's; C.O. "Hayseed" Thomas, Tex Lancaster, Bob Hickman, and Freddie Hickman. We never had any disagreements. Except once!

That was when Al came into the radio station where we were rehearsing for that evening's show and insisted that we add a song called "Blueberries", which none of us had ever even heard of! That was at about 4:30, and our show started at 6pm.

We complained that we didn't know the song, but it did us no good. Al wanted "Blueberries" that evening, and it was his show. At that point we could have cheerfully strangled him!

Anyway, we printed the words REAL BIG on a large cue-card (known as an "idiot sheet") and clipped it on the side of the studio camera. And, as fate would have it, we had a cameraman named Harold Ludwig who loved to torment us. So, he would move the camera in real close and then pull 'way back so that we had to keep leaning forward and strain to read the words. Lean forward and squint and try not to fall on our faces! The viewers must have wondered what was wrong with all of us. Harold would look out from behind the camera and grin.

The song turned out ok, but it was a miracle.

It's really strange what you remember. Mostly, I remember the funny stuff. Cast members Bob and Fred were brothers, and Fred loved to get me laughing while I was singing so I would crackup. Then Bob would get furious with his brother, who swore that he hadn't done anything...he would just look at me with this weird expression on his face and that would be the end of me.

I learned to NEVER look at him while we were being televised.

Of course, in early television, almost nobody did just one thing so while I was being a "person-ality" on Al's Place I was also the receptionist, answering our new Hi-Tech (we thought) switch-board. After a few mishaps, like cutting the boss off in mid sentence, I mastered that little monster and then went on to be the radio log writer for Clay McBride (many of our announcers also did double duty on the WMFD radio station, down one flight of stairs) in the mornings and then rehearse in the afternoon for the show that evening.

Then, in my "spare" time, if the TV station had a blank spot in the afternoon with nothing to fill it I would go upstairs and sing with Johnny Thomas playing the piano. It seems strange now, but I would go from singing "Blue Shadows on the Trail" for Al's show, to "Deep Purple" with Johnny Thomas with hardly a pause in between. In those days you HAD to be versatile because we all held multiple jobs. Somehow, it all worked!

Speaking of Al's Place, the set was a log cabin with rocking chairs and a bench out front and that's what the entire show felt like…a visit on someone's front porch to sing songs and talk.

Actually, Al and Hayseed did the talking while Bob, Fred, Tex and I did the singing.
We never knew what was going to happen. All we rehearsed was our song lineup for that evening and the rest was "whatever will be, will be". We just bluffed it through and acted like that was the way we had planned it.

For a while we also put on a live show on Saturday nights at Thalian Hall and always had a packed house. I know that nowadays we would be considered too corny for words but back in that simpler time, people actually enjoyed us.

I remember those squeaky floorboards in our studio downtown, back when it was WMFD-TV. The studio was on the third floor, and had at one time or another been a dance studio or a skating rink or something else of the sort, and those floorboards really squeaked, so much so that no one was supposed to move around once we were on the air, because you could really hear them.

But during the show one night, I HAD to move. A real sluggish fly was in the studio and Fred was singing a really pretty love song when the fly landed on his nose. He tried to blow it off without being obvious and it would fly off a few inches and then land right back on his nose. This went on during his entire song and, since he was playing the guitar he couldn't use his hands to shoo it away.

And of course our cameraman, being the tormentor that he was, stayed in on a real tight shot. Thank goodness it was nearing the end of the song, because I was laughing hysterically and I MOVED. I'm sure the entire viewing audience heard the resulting squeak!

The funniest thing was…nobody ever said a word about it. It was like it never happened, or it was the most normal thing in the world. Come to think of it, in those days, it was.

Another memory is of Wayne Jackson, running back and forth like a rocket. He was always on the move…I don't believe I ever saw him standing still.

I didn't (and still don't) know anything about the technical parts of television, so I'll leave those stories to the experts. Mostly, I have written about personal things. I do know we had a great group of people who worked together for the ultimate end, whatever that end turned out to be. Luckily, we were the only TV station in this part of the state so there was nothing to compare us to, so we always got lots of mail and rave reviews from the public.

It was a wonderful, if crazy, time and I wouldn't trade it for anything.

With all the problems we had with our inexperience and our make-do equipment we got through it and hopefully, left our imprint on this community. Knowing we put it together and made it work with flour paste and a few straight pins makes the best memories of all.

The gang was all there when the camera rolled. L to R. Tex Lancaster, Bill Hickman, Bob Oman, Twiddle McConkey, Freddie Hickman, and Al Compton, with "Hayseed" Thomas striking a pose in front.

A piece of equipment known as a boom mike allowed sound to be picked up from above. The striped weight shown at the left balanced the mike, and on occasion proved a hazard to crew members who weren't looking where they were going.

Live TV...Expect the Unexpected

Tex Lancaster
Show Host, Musician

Back in the good old days, TV was live. There was no taping of TV shows,(we didn't even know what "tape" was) so whatever happened for there for all the viewers to see!

One time while performing on the "Over at Al's" show, I was standing up while playing my steel guitar. As I was playing, the legs on the guitar started slowly receding to the floor. Nonetheless, I kept playing, hoping that the receding would stop. Well, it didn't, so the cameraman, Dallas Mills, just followed me and my steel guitar all the way to the floor where it finally collapsed. Al Compton commented, "Gaw Dang, he didn't miss a note"!

Another time, after the "Over at Al's" show, we went directly to the Saturday Night Jamboree at Thalian Hall. We had just 30 minutes to go from "Over" to "Jamboree" to be ready to air at 9:00. Just before we were to go on air, I stopped by the men's room, thinking I had enough time before the show but when I was in the bathroom, I heard the opening music start for the live broadcast.

I was to perform the first song, so I rushed up to the stage, grabbed my guitar and ran onstage just in time to start the first verse of Kawlijah. I barely got started singing, when the audience went wild yelling, clapping and whistling. So I thought to myself, "Boy, I must sound real good tonight". Just as I was finishing the first verse, I remembered that I had forgotten to ZIP UP. I told the audience not to leave because I would be right back, ran offstage, zipped, and came back and did the last verse.

That time, the audience really did go wild! Hayseed later told me that he didn't know how I did it and that if it were him, he would have kept right on running and never have gone back onstage!!

When I went to work the next Monday, the first person I saw was Mr. Dunlea sitting in the lobby. He said "Hey Tex, come here a minute". Knowing how Mr. Dunlea was about things like that, I thought to myself, "Well, I guess I'm fired now". Instead, when I got close to him, he started grinning and said, "I heard you had a little accident Saturday Night. I replied, "Yes, I guess I did, Mr. Dunlea". He said, "It happens to everybody". I found out later that he had been listening on the radio and could not figure out what all the cheering was about.

Several months later, I moved into the control room on the audio after the "Over at Al's" show went off the air. Johnny Thomas went out in the studio to do the weather, and just as the camera went on, we discovered he, too, had forgotten to zip up. So, we quickly moved the camera up above his waist and Johnny did the whole weather report with only an "Elvis" shot. Later, I told Johnny, "It happens to everybody".

Another memory of that time was during the 1955 Azalea Festival, the first year that it was ever televised. The way we had to do it seems unreal today. We had one camera with a VERY long cable. We removed the camera from the tripod and lowered it down through the back window of the radio/ tv building on 226 Princess Street to the roof of the McMillan & Cameron Building, which was directly behind the studio and walked it over to the roof of the White Front Grill, which was directly across from City Hall. We set it back up on the tripod. It was amazing to me that we didn't fall through the roof because of the weight of the camera and the age of the roof, but we made it without any injuries. Now that was a remote!

TV commercials and station breaks were all live back then. One day, when we were to do a Su-Ann Shoes commercial, the person from Su-Ann Shoes who was to be on camera came to the studio. She set up her props for the commercial and appeared to be ready to shoot. Just as the camera started rolling, she stood there frozen scared, and suddenly yelled, "I can't do this", and ran off stage. We had to go to a black screen for that one!

One thing about live TV…the only thing you could really expect was the unexpected!

The Rhythm Range Riders get ready for the show to begin Over at Al's

Happy Trails on TV
Esty Davis

I guess it was fitting that my venture into television began at the Green Meadows Saddle Club, since horses and cowboys and country music had always been a big part of my life. During one afternoon there when things must have slowed down a bit, two fellows got to talking about George Deaton's" Six Gun Theater" show that was currently airing at WECT. George was a member of the saddle club, and if he wasn't a real cowboy, he played one on TV, and that was good enough for me.

Esty Davis as "Pan Handle"(left) and Six Gun Theater host George Deaton ham it up for the kids on their popular western comedy and music show

My friend Johnny Leeuwenburg was telling George about a friend of his by the name of Esty Davis (that's me of course) who was in the Army and living in the Wilmington area. Johnny and I had been friends since school and he was real familiar with all my background in show business and often came to see me perform with the likes of Al Fuzzy St John (Lash Larrue's side kick back in the late 40's), Johnny Mc Brown (a well known western cowboy of the day), and Tim Mc Coy (who was a film star almost as famous as Tom Mix or Gene Autry.)

Johnny had been to see us all perform many, many times over all those 20 plus years it had been since we were in school together. I had so many good times back then with those Good Old Boys like Dempsey Watts, Pete Potter, Dave Falk, Billy Shepard, Tex Lancaster, my brother James Davis, Tommy Olyphant, Steve Kelly, Boots Jones, Leroy Pug West. Of course out of all these fine and upstanding local country stars one does shine as he was is now known as Wilmington's King of Country and Southern Rock. This dude even has his very own STAR in our Walk of Fame here in Wilmington. You guessed it folks. It's Charlie Daniels. We had a lot of great times back then.

Well, Johnny really encouraged George to make my acquaintance and possibly get together and create some new ideas for his show. George told Johnny to have me give him a call, which I did right away.

Upon meeting we found many similarities in our ideas. We also found it interesting the fact that we had such diverse backgrounds and educational experiences, George's being very formal and mine of the more practical nature. After many longs hours and much discussion we came up with an idea for a new character. He would be a Baggy-Britches, Bearded, Ten Gallon Hat Wearing son of a Dusty Old Cowboy. This "Fella" was yet to be named and was still in the creative stage.

In the early days of the Six Gun Show we were a daily show airing around 3 to 4 o'clock in the afternoon for the kids in the local viewing area. Later we moved to Saturday mornings. The kids could write to be on the show and we could call out their names and they would then be invited to come on as guests. We also had a bulletin board so that the children could mail in a school picture and we would show them on the air and call them by name and their town and school, and these lucky winners would be named as Official Deputies of the "Six Gun Theater". We sure did get loads of fan mail. I'll bet we made about 25 kids a day Deputy Sheriffs.

We even had a contest where the children were given the chance to name my new character. They were invited to send in their entry with a name they thought best suited this crazy little side kick. The prize for the winner was autographed photo of George and me in costume. We got all kinds of names entered, and for the life of me I can't remember any of them except for the one that stuck like glue right to my baggy britches. Pan Handle had to be it. It looked like me, sounded like me and best of all it fit like a glove. It made me think of Texas and helped me to give a character like "Old Pan Handle" some life.

We sure did have some good times in the early days of television. Along the way as the show's cast began to grow we had lots of funny things happen. Today they call them Bloopers but back then we just left them in, had a good laugh, and everyone had fun. There was not a lot of access to video tape back then so for the most part it was LIVE! ACTION! CAMERA! If you goofed up then it was out there and there was no taking it back.

As I recall one of the first crazy "Bloopers" we had happen was when George and I got the idea to have a shootout that would be more like a real target contest. We were not sure of how to go about this so we took ourselves right down to the local gunsmith who was more than happy to oblige us with his vast knowledge of how to pack a blank. Well folks, we thought we really had something and were going to give the show a big surprise with our new shoot-out contest.

George carefully laid out the plan of how we would be sitting around chewing the fat and telling yarns a mile high, and then one of us would challenge the other to this contest. Suddenly there was the challenge and we both jumped up to pick off these balloons one by one.

George took the lead and reared back, drew his pistol and fired. Kablam! BLAM! BLAM! BLAM! BLAM! BLAM! Six Red Balloons all bit the dust at once as the soap inside them splattered six way to Sunday, killing all my chances to show the world what a good shot "Pan Handle" was, since George had busted all the balloons. I still have to chuckle when I think about the look on George's face that night. He had done what all gunslingers only dream about, but I was just standing there with nothing to do.

As you might guess this little fella "Pan Handle" just had to have his very own horse, a beautiful Appaloosa stallion by the name of 'Doc" to be exact. Boy Howdy, he was a brute and as he was now a TV star he had to have special care and handling. I had a friend by the name of Johnny Davis who was a fine horseman and he often gave me tips on how to care for Doc. Johnny was one of the fellas out at the saddle club and was also an acquaintance of Johnny Leeuwenburg . As we were always trying to find new ways to entertain the children we thought it would make an interesting show to have Johnny come on and tell all about his experiences while growing up around horses. Johnny thought he would tell about how he grew up in Sunset Park across the street from Legion Stadium and how every winter the race horses from up north would be brought there to stay for the winter. They would train the horses there in preparation for the next year and as small boy Johnny got to learn first hand how to care for these wonderful animals. It was these types of shows we liked to share with the kids.

While we were getting the show ready to roll that evening Johnny arrived a little early and I introduced him to George and they hit it off just great. Johnny had brought his costume he had made to wear in the Azalea Festival Parade that was coming up and the group that was in the saddle club were riding in the parade that year. Seeing this, George thought it would be great to have Johnny be a guest on the show that night in his newly fashioned Indian costume. The best I can describe him he was a Seminole-style injun donning a black derby hat with the brim turned down and a feather stuck out of the top, from his long straight black hair down to his moccasin toes he looked injun through and through. George said "What you call yourself there, injun?"

"Injun Joe" Johnny replied, and right then and there the show had a new character.

One night while taping the show," Injun Joe" was giving a rope demonstration of the trick called "The Wedding Ring". He had the rope over his head and was bringing it down over his shoulders to end up with it in a flat spin down near his knees. The plan was to take the spin back up and flip it over his head for a fine finish. George and I were watching closely and the crew was hollering GO! GO! Injun Joe was doing a fine job and impressing us all when all of a sudden he flipped that rope over his head and dogged if that old rope didn't catch ahold of the brim of his hat sending that

hat, feather, and his long black hair flying across the room. It hit the cameraman smack in the head and then landed on top of a chair, looking pretty much like a dead cat wearing a hat.

Now by this time Johnny was heading south saying "boys, just cut that part out." "Sure thing" we replied with a wink. To this day some folks still remember that episode and get a good old laugh just from the thought of it. This experience made such an impression on Johnny he moved to Texas and became a Bull rider.

Now there were many opportunities to have good time around the Six Gun Show. As time went by we added several new characters. As ladies always go first in the cowboy ways I'll tell you about Miss Lela Henderson first up. Miss Lela originally came on the show along with a group of ladies called the Mad Hatters. They danced and sang on early television and as Lela had eyes for Panhandle she approached George about coming on as a regular. Well we talked about it and decided it could be a real cute addition to the cast, so she ended up as a sort of Minnie Pearl type and was always chasing after Panhandle and the two of us had many skits together.

Lela Henderson only had eyes for Pan Handle as she pursued him through many episodes of Six Gun Theater, egged on by "Six Gun" Deaton and a cast of real characters.

I know telling stories about the old days may not mean a whole lot to many of you but there are enough of you out there who remember this show to remember it was good clean fun and it was a learning thing for the kids too. We made such an impression on some kids that even after they grew up they still knew our faces and characters. I fondly recall one evening when my wife Barbara Jean and I were sitting around watching TV when the phone rang. This hasn't been too many years ago, maybe 10 or so. Anyway, I happened to be walking by the phone and picked it up, and a man's voice on the other end asked "Are you Esty Davis, the man who played Pan Handle on Six Gun Theater?"

"Why I sure am, I said. "Who wants to know?"

"Well sir" he said "this is the little boy that adopted you as his grandfather a long time ago. Do you remember me? I lived in Loris, South Carolina." Well I sure do", I said to him. And I sure did, because I remembered getting a letter many, many years ago, the words of a mother who was writing for her four year old son. It really tugged at my heart strings as I read her sweet words about this little fella who had lost his grandfather recently and had asked his mama one day if he could adopt Panhandle to be his new granddad. Well, it wasn't a real "cowboy" thing to do, but I had to go off stage for a minute to compose myself after reading her heartfelt words.

So George and I send him autographed photos and an official looking document making him a special deputy, and mailed them to him and then sort of forgot about it. We figured he was happy and so were we. About a year or so went by and George and I were down in Loris SC doing a personal appearance. I had arrived in street clothes and was carrying my suitcase and heading for the dressing room when a family with a little boy approached me asking "When is Pan Handle going to get here?"

" I am Pan Handle, folks" I said, and the mother whispered, "Please don't disappoint your grandson." Being the real sharp fella that Pan Handle was, I caught on real quick and realized that without the costume the little boy who had adopted me as his grandpa didn't recognize me.

"Oh yes ma'am. If you'll let him come with me I'll take him to find Pan Handle." They obliged and off the two of us went down towards my dressing room. As I began to get my costume together and carefully put each piece on so he could see me becoming his adopted Grandpa he looked up at me and said, " Why, you really are Panhandle!" He grabbed me and gave me a big old hug and as the show was about to start we had to head out to where his parents who were waiting in the hall. This little fella said "No, please let me stay with my Granddaddy."

For a minute we didn't know what to do but then I said I would take him on stage with me and see how he did. Well that little fella stayed right with me the whole show and we sure had a good old time that day.

Now, I was standing there in my kitchen that night after receiving this phone call, talking to this little fella who was now a grown man and reminding me of all those times back then. We talked a long time and he asked if he could come to visit me one day and bring his own son. I was tickled to death to think this young man thought that much of me.

'Why sure", I said. "When do you want to come?" He was in town and so I gave him my address and they came right over. We talked for a long time and I shared with them some pictures and gave the great grandson a little leather pouch of fools gold. He sure was cute and seemed real happy when they left. I haven't heard from them in quite a few years but my hope is that one day the phone will ring and it will be them again and they will bring along a great-great Grandson. Wouldn't that just be something?

Pan Handle and Six Gun George pose in front of the Circle Six Wranglers, another local musical group who made frequent apprearances on Six Gun Theater

As our show became more and more popular we began to be invited to appear at different events. One that I 'specially remember was our trip to the first Blueberry Festival at Elizabethtown. We rode our horses all the way from Wilmington, stopping and resting along the way and being treated like real heroes by groups of folks, including a Boy Scout troop.

As we rode along that morning we made good time as everyone along the way seemed to be bound for the same destination as well. Folks were kinda just scooting on by and we thought to ourselves that there must be a bunch of people headed to enjoy the festival. There was a guest that day scheduled to fly in at the Festival by the name of Dennis Cole and his friend Mary. They were Hollywood movie actors and we guessed that they must have been pretty popular as it was rumored that the officials expected several hundred people to attend the festivities.

Rounding the corner and heading down the main street we began to see some folks and thought we should whoop it up a bit, so we did. Much to our delight they really got a kick out of it and began to applaud and cheer us on so we just kept on riding and shooting and hollering right up to the County Court House steps. For a moment we couldn't believe our eyes. There must have been two thousand people there that day. There stood these Hollywood types and the Mayor ready to greet US and read the proclamation from the City of Wilmington to help celebrate this 1st Annual Blueberry Festival. What a fine day this turned out to be!

Talking about being a team makes me think of just how we all worked hand in hand to make this show really come together. During one of the first few weeks of the show George and I and the boys began to come up with ideas about how to enhance the stage and its backdrops. Since every old western town needs a jail we decided to build us one. So George and I threw some timbers up and before we knew it there was a jailhouse. Pretty soon everyone got into the act and we had folks bringing in props from things they had found out in their barns. Later on when all the dancers started we had a costume department and, well, I guess you might say we had pretty much all the departments like you might think of on today's TV or Movie Sets. Difference was, all the departments were just us, doing whatever needed doing. If I wasn't building and painting something then I even helped with the sewing. Heck, we even had to cut live trees for the set each week. It was just that everyone pitched in and did what needed doing.

There wasn't much technical about any of what we did. We got together, worked hard all week on the sets and props and scripts and music and jokes and the darn thing just came together when it was supposed to. Now don't be fooled. It wasn't always roses but I'll tell you what it was was family and friends and whatever that means to you. It was laughing or cutting up, acting the fool, dancing till you thought you'd drop, singing your old heart out or playing the guitar until your fingers blistered, and smiling all the while. You could sing a hymn like the Old Rugged Cross and it rang true to the heart, and you could tell a joke and slap your knee and do it all in the same 5 minutes and it was ok. This was early TV and we were on an adventure.

You know, when it comes to talking about Six Gun Theater there really is only one name that comes to mind. George Deaton was Six Gun Theater. He was our MC and sang almost every night. He played the trumpet, he was our director, and he really had a hand in every part of this show.

Back in those days it was all about wholesome family entertainment. Our station owner Mr. Dan Cameron was a true southern gentleman with a heart of gold. Whenever we put a skit together or were thinking up an act for the show it was always with due respect for Dan's sensitivity to wholesome entertainment. We were a real team that had been put together by George to have a good time and his charm, talent and charismatic way just made people want to invite you into their homes.

You know they say all good things must come to an end and as fate would have it Six Gun Theater and The George Deaton Show finally came to rest. Six Gun and Pan Handle rode off into the sunset and on the way there, they both began to talk about their individual plans for the future. Remember these two fellows had so many good ideas they had come up with together it was only natural for us to share what was down the road.

George had a hankering for life in Nashville and his plan was to head west and give it his best. He has spent the rest of his career in activities related to show business.

As for Pan Handle, well folks I was a family man as you know and I had already spent my time on the road with many country bands in years past and was eager to stay right here in Wilmington. Life has a funny way of handing you things and as it turns out my life was about to take another turn.

I landed a Pan Handle type role in a small movie, and then came to do another movie called Preacherman, made in Monroe NC. It was a grand experience and opened other doors for me along the way.

And, I got to stay at home here too, because when movie-making came to Wilmington in a big way about 1982, I jumped into it feet-first, so to speak, and spent many years working in the many movies that were filmed here. I know a number of folks from the television field went into the movies and it seemed a real natural thing to do.

You know change is really what it's all about as we all tumble along in life. I think when George and all of us in TV were creating a new idea of entertainment to folks here in this town, we were just part of the bigger picture of what was yet to come on down the road in the field of televison.

At that time we were just working with what we had and giving all we'd got. It's awful funny when you think of what the terms "technical and sophisticated equipment" meant to us back then. Heck, if we had a hammer, some nails, a light and a room big enough for us all to get into and, oh yeah, don't forget the guitar, you can be sure someone would holler "Rolling".

TV Guest to Judge...an Interesting Journey
Gilbert H. Burnett
Chief Judge 5th Judicial District (Ret.)

Although I was never employed by WECT-TV, my association with the station definitely impacted my life and career.

When I returned home after law school as a fledgling attorney I met Ben McDonald, the station's news reporter who had a distinct style and a rather free-wheeling 15 minute news program. At that particular time a court trial of some public interest was underway in Wilmington and after the trial ended Ben asked me to be on his show to explain some of the legal aspects of the case.

One thing led to another and I shortly became a regular on the program, discussing legal matters and interviewing other lawyers and judges. Remember, at that time there had been little opportunity for Wilmingtonians to actually see and hear the members of the judicial system. Somewhat to my surprise, they seemed to be really interested in how the system functioned.

We got lots of letters from viewers with both opinions and questions, and these made good...and sometimes controversial...grist for the TV mill.

Sometimes, though, we ran out of legal topics and I resorted to showing photographs and reading poems...which got mixed reviews.

Ben himself was a real character. He had a rapid fire style of delivery, which I often urged him to "slow down" in order to be more understandable. Once, to make my point, I arrived for the show with a page-long tongue twister which I challenged him to read on the air.

Pushing back the battered fedora (which he always wore during the telecast), he proceeded to read the whole page without a mistake. He looked at me and I said "faster."

He read it faster without getting his tongue twisted, and again I said "faster."

I remember he gave me a look that said he was just humoring me and read it again, speeding it up even more. This time when he gave me that look I said "OK". We never discussed the subject again.

My TV experience led to opportunities that helped shape my career. At one time I invited the president of the N.C. Bar Association to be a guest. This led to being asked to create a television show about legal issues that was shown statewide on Public TV, and this exposure led to membership in the National Bar Committee.

Definitely, I think, the name recognition and credibility gained through local television was an important factor when then Judge Winfield Smith urged me to run for a judgeship.

I feel that having local television that offered a direct outlet for local causes, opinions, and even problems made a real difference, especially at a time when TV was young and local TV even younger.

To that end I have always tried to play it straight with reporters, giving them as much access and information as possible…as long as they played straight with me.

The availability of television access and reporting, I feel, was tremendously important during the racial upheavals of the late sixties and early seventies. It gave both sides an opportunity to be seen and heard, and furnished viewers with facts rather than rumors. Sometimes, just knowing that those involved could go on local TV and air their concerns served to defuse a situation.

Today, I think the general public is much more aware and better educated about our laws and the legal system, thanks largely to television exposure. Of course, given the plethora of programs with law and legal themes, the public still needs to use their own judgment to separate the good from the just plain foolish.

When I think back to the simple sets (a desk and two chairs), the minimal equipment, and the unrehearsed live programs of my early excursions into television, I realize that such unsophisticated beginnings were only the beginning of something really big.

From Parking Lot to Production
...and Beyond
Don Buie

Working for the area's first television station turned out to be a family affair for me, although it certainly wasn't planned that way.

My uncle Jimmy Moore was there first, working as Art Director and almost anything else he was needed for. That's the way TV was then...everybody just did whatever was needed, whenever it was needed.

My uncle was with the station almost from the start, and in 1958 my brother Ken was hired with the photography department. Then, in 1960, when I was a teen looking for work, my uncle got me a job painting stripes in the parking lot when WECT made its move to the present location on Shipyard Blvd. While I was doing this he came out and asked me if I would like a job with the station, which of course I did. So I went inside and talked to Production Manager Roland Register.

He hired me on the spot, although I had absolutely no training, to be a cameraman on a live children's show "Kiddie Time". I must have done ok since shortly afterwards, when one of the film men quit without notice, I was asked to work full time in the film room as a projectionist, while still working in the studio running the teleprompter for the news telecast.

It was while doing this that I worked with newsman Ben McDonald, which turned out to be quite an experience. This brings me to one of the funniest incidents I remember, although it didn't seem so funny at the time.

Ben was scared to death of snakes, and so was I. So during a live newscast one of the studio crew (who will remain nameless) threw a short piece of brown rope across the floor of the set. I swear, it looked just like a snake!

Ben stopped what he was reading, grabbed his stomach, and looked like he was going to throw up. Remember, this was all going out over the air, live! He finally composed himself and continued doing the news. And he never mentioned the incident to anyone, although of course many, many people had seen it happen.

Many viewers who watched WECT during that time probably remember Ben's product called "BMF" which he promoted during his show. (The FCC was a lot more lenient then.) Anyhow, "BMF" stood for Ben McDonald's Formula…or maybe "Ben's Magic Formula", since it was a salve supposed to promote hair growth…and Ben was bald!

Before each show Ben could be found in the man's room applying black shoe polish to the little bit of fuzz he could find on his head. Then, as the show was ending he would take off the old hat he always wore and proudly point out how much hair "BMF" was growing for him. I think sometimes he actually believed it himself.

The saddest moment, and one I will always remember, was the plane crash during the air show WECT was sponsoring. Along with members of the military aboard the plane were members of our staff.
We were actually filming the plane as it took off. I was carrying a wireless transformer for Wayne Jackson's mike, and we were actually out on the field so that Wayne could interview the members of the Blue Angels parachute team when they landed after jumping from the plane.

Wayne and I were among the first to get to the burning crash site, and I will never forget the sight and sound. God bless all who lost their lives, and thank God for all who survived it.

Uncle Jimmy, Ken and I stayed with WECT-TV for many years, learning to handle the changes in technology and equipment as they came along. I became Film Director and then went on to become Studio Director/Switcher. I am now 60 years old and look back on my TV career as being some of the best years of my life.

Film was edited, spliced and joined before airing

Right...there was nothing like a television camera to attract all the kids in the neighborhood. Here Don esplains how it works while he sets up for an outdoor shot.

Below: From highschool to a director's job, Don Buie,shown here in the early sixties, operates the Switcher from the control room while a live show is in progress in the studio.

Above: General Mgr. Claud O'Shields wielded the shovel at ground breaking for WECT's new home on Shipyard Blvd. Among those looking on are C.D. Martin, WECT sales manager, New Hanover County Commission Chairman Alex Hall, WECT engineers Bill Elks and Ed Herring, and Wilmington Mayor J.E.L. "Hi Buddy" Wade

As the station was being built the new microwave tower went up, linking the studio with the Delco transmitter and WECT with network programming via WNCT-TV in Greenville. Unpredictable and subject to outages, it was the best method available at the time. It also gave rise to the joke that WECT stood for We Expect Constant Trouble.

The "Art" of Television
Bebe Bryant
Art Director - 1961-1964

Bebe Bryant

Little did I realize what the future held for me that day back in 1961! I had recently returned from Charlotte, N.C. to the place that I called home, Wrightsville Beach, N.C., with my two preteen children after my marriage of fourteen years had come to an end. I was equipped with a high school education, a correspondence course in art, and little else except raw nerve, and that was a bit frayed.

As I pondered our future, I realized that starting over was not going to be an easy task. Having been a wife and mother for fifteen years, I had mastered the art of home-making, which involved gourmet cooking, landscaping, interior decorating, fashion design and creating clothes. One would think that these talents should surely count for another 'degree' of sorts from the University of 'hard knocks'.

Upon hearing of a job opening for an Art Director at WECT Television, I bravely made the call to schedule an appointment, and was told the interviews were being conducted from ten until one that week. The next day found me in the lobby of the television station bright and early, sitting quietly among and observing the other applicants. Overhearing their qualifications and various degrees of experience, I felt like bolting out of the door, but was restrained by thoughts of my responsibilities and the future for my children, as well as myself.

With much trepidation, I entered the office of Claud O'Shields, station manager, and quipped that "I might not qualify for this position". Mr. O'Shields commented "We're not necessarily looking for someone with a degree". As the interview proceeded, I was told they were looking for a well-rounded individual who could adapt to any situation and this seemed right down my alley. I felt better knowing there truly might be a chance for me.

We began the second half of the hour by going on a walking tour of the areas that would be involved directly with the position of the art director. The first office was that of Bobby Gurganious, Promotions and Copy, and her excellent work was then delivered to the office of Bill Elks, Operations Manager. The next office was that of Bob West, Production Manager. Mr. West was to be my immediate supervisor, and written orders were to come directly from him. No assignments were to begin on artwork or sets without direct written instructions from Mr. West.

The most important areas consisted of two rooms which were used by Phil Morgan, Photography Department, and two rooms which were used by the Art Department. The largest of the art rooms was where a variety of props or sets were constructed and stored when not in use. This area was also used for storing items used for commercials. I observed cans of paint, ladders, and various items of furniture, and other things that the merchants wanted used to promote their wares. It was, in fact, a hodge-podge of practically everything.

The Studio was the largest of the rooms and especially interested me. Here was where the 'action was', just as I saw it on my television at home. I felt I had truly arrived into the 'World of Television' this day!

Standing there in the studio, to my left was the set of the Jim Burns Show as well as various others used for News, Sports & Weather, etc. Directly in front of me was the set for the Ben McDonald Show. Seeing them all together like this all in one big room, I had to admit that it wasn't "exactly" what I saw on the TV at home.

I saw cameras on wheels being operated by the cameramen, and I noticed that one of the cameras was focused on the 'art cards' standing on easels. I also noticed the ingenious and somewhat basic backdrops. Creating these would soon be my job!

The artist was expected to design, paint and, usually, build a variety of studio sets and props . Here, Bebe works on "Bebe's Weather Beacon"

110

I stood amazed and excited to be witnessing the real 'guts' of live television for the first time…what a show to a novice! Nothing appeared to be more than I could 'learn to handle' because it seemed to be calling out to me, and I was encouraged by the feeling.

As we completed the tour we returned to the Art Department where a more in-depth review was given to its contents and the total responsibility for this department. The Line-O-Scribe machine was a type-setting machine to be used for small, quick signs. A drawer was filled with various types of rub-off letters, and there was a large tank that was used for air-brushing jobs. A 4'x 8' piece of upson board was used as a giant slanted art board, to be for large stand-up work. Underneath this were various-sized pieces of art cards.

At the end of the room was a smaller, semi-flat table easel with a chair (the only one in the room) where sit-down, in-depth artwork was done. Shelves in this area held various sizes of lettering brushes and pens. I was shown a large stack of 11" x 14" art cards in several tones of gray, and some were totally black. Once these cards were rendered, they were covered with a thin piece of overlay to protect all work done.

There were two file cabinets stacked one on top of the other that warehoused all of the original treasured 11" x 14" cards. These cards included the WECT Station ID cards, as well as all cards used for the merchant-sponsored television spots on the air. These cards represented thousands of dollars for the station, and thousands of hours of artwork as well. I quickly realized the importance of the role of Art Director in the total realm of the production end of things. I later learned that before my employment, many assignments had been contracted out to printers, artists, or whoever could cover the assignments, but because these were often needed literally at a moment's notice, this hadn't proved to be a good way to do things.

I watched Phil Morgan in Photography, taking photos of the art work on the 11 x 14 cards. He had folded the protective sheet of paper to the underside, placed the card flat on the table, and with an overhead camera, snapped the picture. He explained that all art work on these cards had to be made into slides which were then loaded into a revolving slide drum. They were to be programmed on schedule; some were slides of the sponsor, station information, station ID, etc. These cards were important pieces of original work, and were kept filed safely in the Art Department until needed. The art cards were kept in the Photography Department in case slides needed to be replaced for any reason.

My personal tour ended back in Mr. O'Shield's office where he handed me three blank cards, several brushes, and jars of black and white paint. My assignment was to design three WECT Station ID cards and return within a week. WECT was the only television station in the region in 1961. Color television was on the horizon, but had yet not arrived; this was the reason artwork and sets were done only in tones of gray.

Needless to say, I slept very little the next five nights, and spent the days doodling, sketching, and discarding scraps of paper, as well as cast-off ideas. Not daring to put a mark on the three cards, I finally 'bit the bullet' and rendered my designs on the sixth day. I carefully covered the three cards with a clear, protective piece of paper, remembering the special care the cards had been given at the station, and placed them in a file folder for easier handling.

Studio logos and other ad art were painted on cards and set before the camera

I returned to the lobby with the same group of hopeful applicants, and noticed them carelessly handling their cards, which were not protected with any type of covering whatsoever. Fortunately, two of my best traits were a photographic memory and the care and neatness in the way with which I handled my cards. I submitted my cards, had a brief conversation with Mr. O'Shields, and was told I would receive a call regarding their decision.

Even though the children and I stayed busy registering them for their new schools, walking on the beach, and adjusting to our new life, the next days seemed long, as if time was standing still while I waited on a call from the station. The call finally came, and I was overjoyed to learn that I had been chosen for the job, and was to report for work the next week on a thirty-day trial basis.

I immediately felt at home with a very special group of people. It seemed as if I had joined a close-knit family, and still think of them as such even today. Time flew by. The thirty-day trial period ended, I was given a raise, and was told that I was 'there to stay'. I was ecstatic, to say the least, at the opportunity that had been afforded to me.

I settled into my job as Art Director, and the next three years at WECT were to become the most challenging of my thirty-two years. I definitely had entered into fascinating work in the world of television! I felt fortunate to be among such a special group of people where cooperation and respect between each and every department was of the utmost importance. I can honestly say that no two days were ever the same for me during the entire time with WECT, and I was never bored with my job.

My duties covered the full array of television art which included layout and design for studio cards and all the pieces of artwork that went to the Photography Department, where they were then turned into slides. My duties were to supply newspaper and magazine ads and to execute promotional posters, ads and cards. Other responsibilities varied from set designs and decorating, to all phases of artwork and lettering for slides and studio cards. I gained the respect of all the men, rarely saw the girls, and proudly earned the position of being 'one of the boys'.

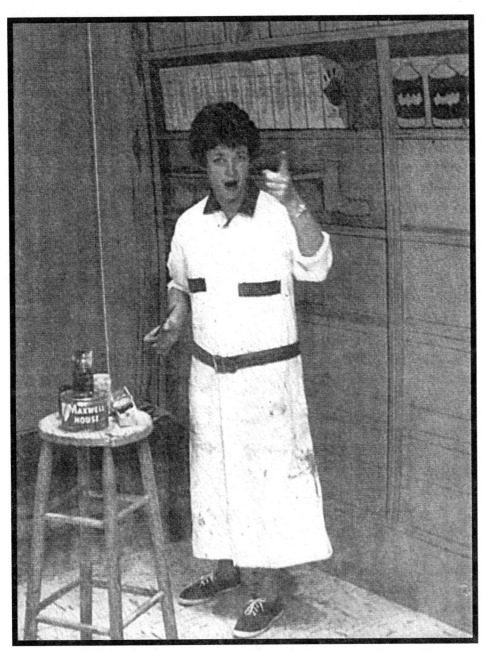

Everyone in those days ad-libbed through a lot of situations, and I managed to 'fly by the seat of my pants' at times in order to see all projects through from start to finish. It was always a new challenge and an opportunity for growth for me daily.

In those days no one had learned "TV Art" in school, and there was really no place to look up instructions, so it was just a case of taking everything you knew and applying it to the special demands and restrictions of creating art work that would look good through the lens of a camera.

And, there was the added pressure of having to sometimes come up with a new logo or design for a commercial on very short notice.

Don't touch the wet paint!! Large sets were often built and painted right in the studio. Touch-ups were often needed

113

From the written orders, I was given a specific number of weeks to design the more difficult sets, and oftentimes to create the idea as well as the finished product. The ideas and designs for these project came at the strangest times, often in the middle of the night. Some of the results were truly unique!

This news set was a good example of ingenuity. While Bill Smith reported, the globe behind him slowly turned, hand cranked by a crew member just off camera. How fast it turned sometimes depended on the energy of the man at the crank.

The responsibilities grew and, as with almost everyone else, began to include many things that didn't necessarily "go with my job, including being in front of the camera as well. I began to fill in as one of the guests on the Jim Burns Show when he needed an extra person on short notice. This experience allowed me the `best seat in town' and gave me the chance to meet an endless array of celebrities, public officials, and people from all walks of life.

My reputation spread as a local artist, giving me the opportunity to design the sets for four years for the local Azalea Festival pageant. These were the years when the pageants were 'Royal and Big'.

When called upon, I modeled clothes, shoes, and other products. I joined the Carolina Farm Beat Show as a co-hostess with Ben McDonald. The show was pre-recorded in the afternoons to be aired the next morning, something rather out-of-the ordinary for live television! Since Ben was a flamboyant and somewhat unpredictable person, this proved to be quite an experience.

Double Duty...staff artist Bebe Bryant models an elegant Azalea Festival ball gown on the Jim Burns Show

At one point, I was asked to design a weather set which was to be called 'Bebe's Weather Beacon.' I had enjoyed all of my work experiences up until then; all types of art, modeling, and being a co-hostess, but with no mechanical or technical knowledge, I balked at the request to host the weather show. My trips to the weather station to 'learn the weather' were futile, and the show was discontinued upon my insistence after it aired several times. It was not my cup of tea at all !

Salary increases were few and far between. Even though I was recognized as 'one of the boys', my pay scale classically reflected that I was paid as 'one of the girls'. At that time, females were not compensated at the same rate as the males, even though their duties and responsibilities were the same, or sometimes more.

Sadly, I resigned in 1964 to undertake more lucrative ventures and to be able to put my efforts into building my own business. But, I will always consider my days at WECT, forty years ago, truly the 'good ole days', and still remember them freshly and fondly today.

Wayne Jackson and Bebe discuss the fine points of TV art on the Jim Burns Show

WECT - A Great Place to Start

Jackie Pastis Margoles

In the early 1960's, I was 20 years old and was very assured of my career goals. Most of my friends were showing off engagement rings after attending college for only two years. What a payoff! But the mentality in those years was to look for a husband in college, instead of a career..

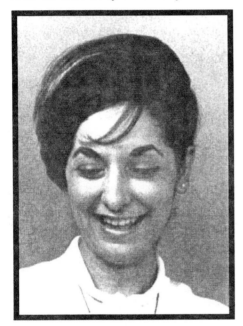

Jackie Pastis Margoles

But this was not the career path I wanted. I wanted more than just taking care of my future mate. I couldn't see myself in pearls, high heels and an apron as my husband walked in from a hard day at the office. "Leave it to Beaver" was what the perception was of the dutiful wife. My daughters laugh at that persona today, but that's the way it was ... like it or not.

My sight was focused on Shipyard Blvd, the new home of WECT television. Those days it was on-the-job training because television was so new that there was really no place you could go to learn it. That is why creativity was so rampant; there were no rules or restrictions on what could be done but one thing always remained on top of the list ...everything had to be tastefully portrayed. My first job after interviewing with Dan Cameron was as the station's receptionist.

I was thrilled but reality soon reared its ugly head when many of the calls I took were asking bizarre questions about their favorite soap opera stars. Many callers believed that if you worked in television all the stars were right there in the station. We actually got some bomb threats if we interrupted their shows. The phone lines would become flooded with calls of angry viewers asking why the President had to speak during their shows.

I soon got promoted to the Traffic Department. That was the heart and soul of the television format, because there we had to keep exact documentation of what went on the air for every minute of every hour. I mean, every second had to be accounted for! I worked with Cornelia Luweenburg Royal. Our office was the first one a visitor saw as they made their way back to the studio and quite a few famous persons stopped to say hello. My favorite was when Michael Landon was in town for the azalea festival. Landen (Little Joe) was so much fun to talk to and without any "diva" airs that from then on we faithfully watched Bonanza..

117

George Tregembo from the "Totem In Zoo" was a regular on our programming. He was always stopping by with strange and exotic animals. One day one of his snakes escaped and slithered under the door into our office.. Corny and I jumped up on the window ledge and screamed so loudly that the snake hid in a corner of our office. Corny got a big laugh because I lost one shoe when I made my jump.

Jim Burns was always in our office to bum cigarettes from Corny ("Boobsie") as he called her. We always say Jim should have left at least $5,000 in his will for Corny to pay for all the cigarettes he borrowed. We still laugh at that today. To say that Jim was frugal was an understatement.

Corny was always the most giving and fair person I ever knew. She would never say "no" to anyone that needed help. She is still my lifelong friend whose friendship I cherish to this day, and she continues helping people through her church.

I soon started doing commercials for Belk-Berry, The Cotton Council of America, Holsum Bread, and Goldings, among others. My favorite commercials were with Gar Faulkner and his innovative Cooperative Savings and Loan. The commercials all had a cloak and dagger air to them, with me wearing a trench coat and a slouch hat.

Then my big break on the air arrived. I was teamed with John Stikes to host WECT's and Winn-Dixie's daily half-hour bingo game. This was the first audience-participation game show in our coverage area, and it was instantly a big hit. Over 25,000 new cards were distributed weekly at banks and grocery stores.

People would win cash prizes when they filled their bingo card. They seemed to love the idea that they could win money and at the same time hear their names called out on TV.

It was lots of fun and I quickly became known as the Bingo Lady .Today I am much less enthusiastic about that name, but at the time I felt like it was star billing.

Jackie Pastis and John Stikes look over the hundreds of cards sent in by viewers trying to win prizes on Zingo Bingo, WECT's first audience-participation game show.

118

The game drew thousands of viewers competing for the "big" cash prizes

The Azalea Festival parade was covered live each year by WECT. I was co-host with Jim Burns and Bill Smith for four fun filled years. Narrating a parade is not an easy job since most of what you say is strictly ad lib. After all, how many different ways can you describe a marching band? And sometimes the unit you see marching up the street toward you is NOT the one you have been given information about.

Burns would read the float's name, which often did not correspond to the parade line-up we had been given before air time, and I would fluff up the description of each float. One year at the end of the parade Jim looked at me and asked me to describe what the "long wide load" float coming down the street was about.

I looked at Jim with crossed eyes and said "Goodbye, Jim". I never let him forget that one.

My mentor and confidant was always Bobbie Marcroft, God rest that talented soul. She was an exquisite writer for all the on-air copy. Dot Romeo was also a wonderful mentor for me. She always had wise advice on life and boyfriends. She is my "aunt" and I love her dearly. In 34 years of my married life she has never forgotten my entire family's birthdays.. Her cards have never stopped coming.

The day came when I was offered a job at Metro-Media WTTG television in Washington, D.C., a great career opportunity that I just couldn't turn down. The station threw a wonderful going away party for me. I was presented with a silver box and a corsage made of dollar bills that totaled $10.00 . I wore it proudly on the flight to Washington. Do you think I could safely wear money on my shoulder today? I don't think so.

I look back on my days at WECT with wonderment and joy. There could not have been a better place to learn about a new and growing media. In those creative days you could write, produce and perform your own commercials. Then, we worried about the correct spelling or punctuation on a crawl, and the copy was written to inform and enlighten the public, not to create shock, horror and embarrassment.

In those days, your television set was the altar of your home, with the whole family watching. Would you have invited any individual into your home that constantly used the "f" word in conversation or stripped naked in front of your family? You all know the answer to that! I just miss the days of continuity acceptance in copy which kept such garbage from coming in. Today, I'm afraid the "envelope had been stretched" until there is almost no envelope left.

It was a great ride at WECT and I treasure every moment.

Jackie usually narrated the parade, but this time she rode...as a mermaid

From Paint Brushes to Pixels
Ron Hawes
Art Director

When I started at TV6 in September 1969, I was an assistant to the art director, Mrs. Penny Rogers. Back then there were no computers, no Adobe Photoshop, no floppy disks, no CDs, no e-mail, NO NOTHING. All the artwork we did was done BY HAND. About after a year I came to TV6, Penny left and I became art director.

When I think back to the way I did artwork then and the way I do it now, there is no comparison.

Back in those "early days", I had a large angled drawing table with a place to store my brushes, small jars and tubes of paint, drawing pens and ink. In the corner of my office there was a machine that made signs or as we called them back then, "art cards". This "Line-A-Scribe" sign machine had several racks of wooden and lead type and numbers of different sizes and styles.

No pixels, just paint and print for Ronnie Hawes in 1969

When I got an order for some artwork for a commercial and it called for a sign or signs (art cards) to be made I would set the letters on the machine inside a predrawn TV template. Now remember, all the type was made backwards so when it was printed, it came out readable.

You set up letters from right to left, locked the type into place and then applied colored oil based ink over the letters with a small handheld rubber roller. Insert a 11 x 14 inch colored card face down, roll a roller that presses the card onto the type and back, lift up the card, sprinkle drying powder on the type to dry the ink and you're done.

After some time of doing signs backwards, I got pretty good at reading signs and billboards in my car's rear view mirror.

But, sometimes mistakes happened; a misspelled word, a wrong date or time. Whether it was the client's fault or my fault, the whole card had to be done over again. No just hitting the "delete" key and starting afresh.

Then came the fun part, cleaning all that type after each use. That's a story in itself.

When it came to cutting out pictures of cars, clothes and other things for commercials, I would use an X-Acto knife… sometimes blood was spilt, those little blades were sharp! At times the paper was hard to cut or the paper would tear and I would have to put it back together so it wouldn't show on TV. Now that was fun!

My favorite part of the job, I think, was drawing or painting original cartoons or illustrations for a commercial. Most of the time the client liked what I designed for their TV spot, but every now and then... its the wrong color, or the face on the cartoon character wasn't happy enough or, now get this, the clouds I did didn't look right to the client. They looked right to me...but.

If you had to paint over a portion of a cartoon, at the client's request, sometimes the paint would mix and you would have to do that part, if not the whole card, all over again. Sometimes, after all the work I went through, I had visions of putting my hands around the client's neck and...

By the way, at that time the usual way to use these cards was to put them on tripod stands in the studio and while the camera whirred away, they were either carefully removed one by one to reveal the commercial, or the camera panned down a line of them resting on a number of stands. The problems came if somehow the cards were out of sequence or, heavens forbid, some of them tipped over and fell down. There was never a dull moment with live TV.

I remember painting a large board that depicted one side of an apartment building. This was for a commercial about TV antennas, and it had windows that would actually open. Several other employees and I were recruited to do the commercial. Every time I would open my window, I would have a pie thrown at my face. Not only was this fun and messy, but tasty too.

I guess one of the oddest requests I got for some artwork was when one of the female employees who worked in engineering wanted me to paint a sunflower on her navel. OK. She was tall and had long blonde hair. It was during an Azalea Festival when she came to my office to have her naval adorned.

While I was painting her navel (and enjoying it) two elderly women who were waiting to be on The Jim Burns Show saw me painting a woman's belly button. Our eyes met! Not a word was spoken. Their eyes were as big as saucers and their mouths, wide open. I don't think I'll ever forget the look on their faces. They looked as if I was committing some kind of sin.

It was about the mid 80's when I got almost hi-tech. I got a kind of electronic sign machine, and a large floor camera that could take pictures of your artwork. You would make a sign by pushing buttons for each letter and it would come out black letters on a strip of white film, which you could then cut and place the way you wanted for signs on white paper. Then, put it in the camera, load film sheet, take picture, develop film. Film would be black and letters, logos or illustrations would be clear. Then you turned over the film and painted on back of the film to add color.

Early television made up in ingenuity and imagination what it may have lacked in efficiency!

In April 1989, I got my first computer. With it you could draw, "paint", type out signs, it was great, I loved it. Several years later Daniel Norris, who is my supervisor, and I got better computers with Adobe Photoshop. Now when I do artwork of any kind, I do it in layers. That means that each part of your work can be done separately and then saved.

If anything needs to be changed, just change that layer you want changed without having to do the whole thing over. This is also true for making signs. There are many styles of letters, or fonts, to choose from, any color you can think of. You can do many special effects with letters like two-tone colored letters, drop shadows, outlines and much, much more. Nowadays, almost anything that the imagination can conceive can be brought to life on your computer.

Drawing cartoons and illustrations are a lot of fun on the computer. Cutting out pictures is so much easier and faster, no knife to use, no more blood letting. I can also scan photographs, logos and the like, fix them up on the computer, make them look better than they were before I got them. After each assignment, I then "electronically send" the graphics I did to one of two rooms where they put commercials together or I send them to the production control room for editing.

How far we've come from those art cards falling off their tripods!

On a shelf in my office near my two-monitor computer, there is a coffee mug with an old TV6 logo. In that mug are a few brushes, pens and a few other things I used years ago. When I look at those things and then see what I have in my office now, I wonder how I ever got things done. But I did.

Do I miss the "old way" I did graphics back then? Not really. Instead of using a paintbrush, I now use a mouse. Instead of setting type, I just type letters on the screen, color included. Doing computer graphics today is easy, fast and fun.

In the 33 years I've been at WECT, I've seen many changes in the way we do things like news, weather, sports, sales, commercial production and other things. When I came to TV6, I did artwork the old fashioned way - by hand. Now it's by computer. Oh, by the way, we now use the word graphics to describe artwork. Come to think of it, I can't remember the last time I heard the word "artwork".

Wonder what the next 33 years will be like at WECT-TV6? We can only imagine.

This was probably not in their job descriptions. Jim Burns, Bob West and Wayne Jackson take their on-the-air duties outdoors to go elephant riding

Remembering James Moss (Jim) Burns

For many years, the voice and face of Jim Burns was one the public closely associated with WECT. From 1958 until 1986, he was an almost inseparable part of the public image of the station.

His noon-time talk show, always done live, offered an opportunity for civic groups, institutions and individuals to showcase their causes to a larger audience than they could have reached in any other way. Whether the topic was education, charity, arts, politics, or how to bake a better apple pie, his show was an open forum.

Early on, Jim had mastered that important skill of asking the guests a few pertinent questions and then letting them do the talking.

During his years on the air, an appearance on the Jim Burns show by Azalea Festival celebrities was an expected part of the festival schedule. From movie stars to Teen Age Princesses…all were treated with an equal degree of importance.

There were some regular guests who could be counted on to show up at an almost minute's notice when someone else couldn't make it; the master Italian chef who always arrived with an array of goodies, the herpetologist who brought his live snakes (of which Jim was deathly afraid but usually managed to maintain his cool), and artists of all sorts who welcomed any opportunity to display their talents.

As was the case in TV's earlier days, no one was hired to do just one thing, so Jim did station breaks and commercials, and was also the weatherman.

This was long before forecasters had to be degreed meteorologists, before electronic graphics, and such technical marvels as moving three-D cold fronts and triple Dopplers were unheard of.

So, the weatherboard was rudimentary, to say the least. At first it was a large blackboard with outlines of the coverage area map on which temperatures and other such information were written in chalk. Later a short-lived experiment involved a magnetized board which pivoted, with a coverage area map on one side and a state map on the other. Metal-backed numbers and symbols were then stuck on in the appropriate places.

But the trouble with this was that, unless the board was pivoted very slowly and smoothly, said numbers and symbols tended to fall off. It takes a lot of aplomb to keep on smiling and talking when the temperature has quite literally plummeted… onto the floor.

Jim Burns and his short-lived "magnetic" weather board

It was probably a sort of weird recognition of Jim's local celebrity when he became the target of a stalker, long before this sort of thing was accepted as a scary part of being a public figure.

An emotionally disturbed woman was convinced that Jim was sending her coded and very personal messages along with the weather forecasts and began writing him long, ardent, but nutty letters. She even convinced a gullible car dealer to charge the purchase of a new auto to Jim and finally, showed up at his home one evening armed with a meat cleaver.

A call to the police resulted in getting the woman the help she needed, but afterwards Jim read his fan mail with a newly wary eye.

Jim Burns was a unique person. In his spare time he was a master gardener and a world traveler. He could on occasion be a hard taskmaster, and was known around the station for his frugality. But he could also be a charming host, an attentive ear, and an unflappable on-the-air presence.

Jim left WECT in 1986 after a change in ownership, and died in 2002. He is still remembered by many older viewers as the face, and voice, of WECT.

Jim interviews Mayor O.O. Allsbrook as the mayor cuts the ribbon for the grand opening of the Sears store in Hanover Center

Jim Burns chats with reporter Kliest Wideman on the set of his noon time show

A Happening Place To Be
Robert Rogers

In the early sixties, WECT-TV was a happening place to be and I was happy to be there. Here I was, working with people I grew up watching on television; Ben McDonald, Bob West, Wayne Jackson and Jim Burns. I was young with a strong desire to be a still photographer and considered myself lucky to get a job at the station working in the photo lab in the afternoons and in film projection in the evenings.

Processing and printing black and white still photos was something I knew how to do. However, processing black and white negative 16mm movie film was something else. I was responsible for processing the news film for the six o'clock and the eleven o'clock news in a temperamental film processor that was less than three feet long.

I also learned to edit news film for continuity. Our editing equipment consisted of two hand crank rewinds, a small viewer, optical sound reader and a film splicer. When I started shooting news film, I learned to edit in the camera for those times when that was all the editing we had time for. There were the times when film for a late breaking story went straight from processor to the projector. I loved the pressure and excitement of making it happen.

The film was electronically switched to a positive image and shaded by the engineer when it went on the air. Two engineers I remember well are Cliff Snow, who was always rushing between the tape machine and the control room, and Ed Herring who never rushed anywhere but always took care of business.

My shift as projectionist started after the six o'clock news. We had two film projectors in a dark projection room adjoining the control room. The projectors faced each other with a set of mirrors evenly spaced between them so that one of the mirrors was always in position to reflect the projected image into a small video camera set at a ninety-degree angle to the projectors. The director in the control room was responsible for running the projectors and switching the mirrors to the correct projector.

It was my responsibility to make sure the correct film was loaded based on the log sheet and to tell the director what projector the film was on. Three directors I remember working with were Bruce Gibson, Dan Brinson and Ken Buie. Ken's brother Donnie, who I was in high school with, taught me how to edit and run the film projectors.

We had a couple of monster two-inch videotape machines, but most of the national commercials and some of our evening programming went on the air from those projectors so I had a pretty heavy responsibility. With only two projectors, things could get a little dicey when we had four film commercials in a break. After some practice, I could thread a projector in eight seconds. I would stand by the projector that was running with my hands in the ready position and a ten second commercial on a plastic reel clenched in my teeth. When the other projector started and the mirrors switched, I quickly loaded the third commercial on that projector, rushed around to the other projector so when that one stopped, I could repeat the process.

High tech it wasn't, but it worked pretty well most of the time. If we were running a film program on one projector, I spliced the commercials together to run on the other projector. That wasn't nearly as challenging or as much fun.

When I finally got the opportunity to wind up a Bell & Howell movie camera and shoot news film, I knew what direction I wanted my photography career to take. Phillip Morgan, who was the chief photographer when I joined the station, was a patient man and a good teacher. I learned a lot from Phillip about still and motion picture photography. We developed a friendship (no pun intended) that lasted for many years: Mark Venters took over as chief photographer when Phillip left. I didn't have enough experience at that time to get the job.

We were the only game in town and we were learning as we went because there was nobody else to learn from. We were a small group of people that shared a common goal and we knew how to party. The parties always evolved into a Greek dance fest with Jackie and Dorothy Pastis leading the rest of us in the dance. Those were great times. It didn't matter if you were an on the air personality or the weekend projectionist: We were all the same on the dance floor.

One day that I remember vividly was November 22, 1963. I was standing over a hot film processor when someone walked by the lab on the way to the control room and said that the president had been shot: By the time I got in the control room, a group of people were huddled in front of the network monitor with shocked faces, some with tears in their eyes. It was like the whole world had stopped. When an emotional Walter Cronkite announced that the president was dead, people were sobbing out loud. I remember Jackie Pastis was almost physically sick from the shock of what we had just heard. It is a day I will never forget.

I left WECT for a job as a full fledged news photographer with WRAL-TV in Raleigh and from there to WFMY in Greensboro where I did news photography and documentaries and then back to WRAL where I directed sports features and commercials: In 1969 I joined Jefferson Pilot Broadcasting in Charlotte where I helped organize a film production company to produce national and regional commercials. I shot and directed for Jefferson until the fall of 1973 when I started my own film production company shooting and directing commercials and documentaries.

We have come light years in technology since I worked at WECT. However, I was fortunate to start my career there when the business was young, the technology simple and mistakes were forgiven because we were all learning together. My tenure at WECT started me on a career path that might not have been possible had it not been for Bob West who hired me and my friend Phillip Morgan who shared his knowledge of photography.

It was a magic time and place for me. Thank you.

Local Color Comes To Channel 6

The WECT-TV control room went through a complete revamping when studio color cameras, color film projection system and color video tape was added to make Channel 6 a complete color station.

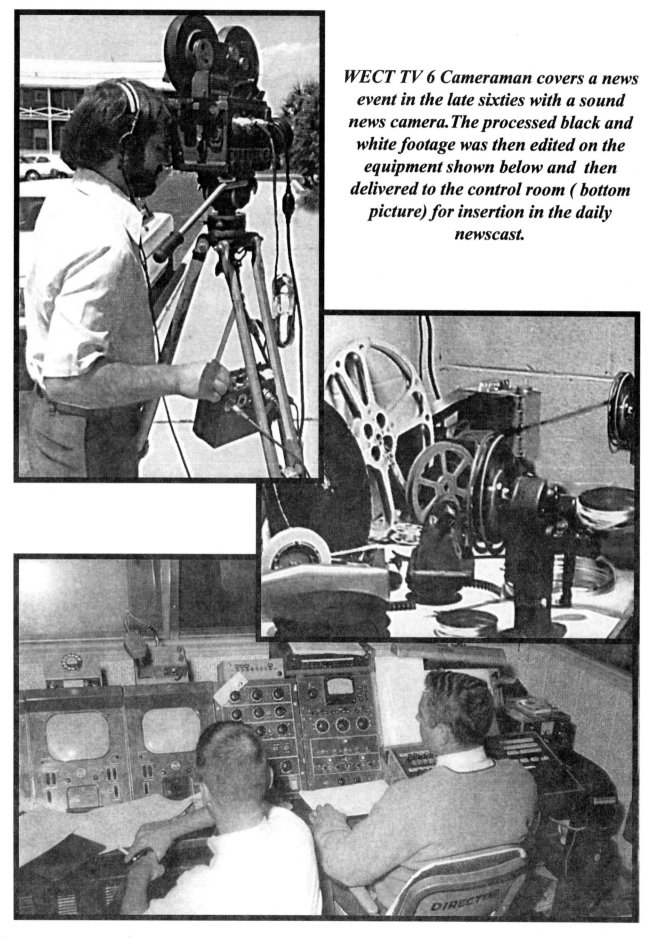

WECT TV 6 Cameraman covers a news event in the late sixties with a sound news camera. The processed black and white footage was then edited on the equipment shown below and then delivered to the control room (bottom picture) for insertion in the daily newscast.

Newswomen and
The Crime and Violence Beat
Betty Hutson Perkins
News Department, 1964-1973

In 1964, I made the big leap from print journalism to television. True, in 1964 TV was not still in its infancy, but it was definitely struggling with puberty.

To those involved at that time, it seemed to be the highest of high tech. Looking back, it was little beyond the concept of two tin cans and a string. We simply didn't know that we couldn't possibly do the things we wanted to do with what we had...so we just went ahead and did it anyhow.

The News Department in 1965 consisted of Ken Murphy and myself, along with a sports reporter and a weatherman. It's a good thing the staff wasn't any bigger, since our "office" was a converted supply closet little more than an arm's-span wide. If one of us wanted to push back our chair to stand up, we had to get an all-clear from the other to avoid a mid-room collision.

I remember the big technical leap, early on, when our manual typewriters with the big type were replaced with...gasp!. electric ones.

At first, my job was to rewrite the news from the AP machine and the "handouts", do some telephone interviews, and write the script for the 6 O'Clock News.

However, before long I became the first female beat reporter, print or TV, in southeastern North Carolina. True, there were already some females here doing "news" but they were confined to what was considered "women's stuff". They read some news on the air, but none had yet been sent out into the field to cover crime, violence, wrecks, fires, and the other events that had been considered "men's work."

Over the years I have read many stories of the hardships, opposition, and other general meanness encountered by women trying to break into formerly masculine fields. Let me say that I ran into very little of that. Most other reporters, politicians, city officials and so on were at the least nonthreatening, and often even helpful. Partly, I guess, this was due to the surprise that I was there at all.

I do remember, however, one nose-to-nose encounter with Police Chief "Fats" Williamson. During a news conference to announce a new police "ride-along" program allowing reporters to ride patrol with cops, he added that this was available to everyone except Reporter Hutson who, because of her sex, could only go with a chaperone.

The discussion that followed got rather heated…I won.

Later, the Chief and I became good friends and his only reservation about my work was his frequent observation that I was "going to get myself killed" out there. And, just as a note, let me say that I have never known a law enforcement official, anywhere, anytime, who was more concerned about his city, his men, and their welfare.

Now, female news reporters are the norm and are expected to go anywhere, under any circumstances. I have always felt that women make good reporters because they are usually more observant, more intuitive, and people seem to be more open with them.

Over the years they have shown that they don't expect any special treatment, and have learned not to care if their makeup has worn off and their hair is stringy from the mist from the firemen's hose. It's the story that matters!

In those early days of my television career, reporters usually did not have a photographer to go along on an assignment. You did it yourself. I will always remember my first Bell and Howell camera, which Wayne Jackson shoved into my hands and said "Here. Learn to use this."

"This" was a chunk of battleship grey metal that could have knocked down an elephant. Only motion, no sound, and the film was wound with a big attached key. You had to try to time your film segments to the length of time it would keep grinding before running down. It made for some interesting editing later.

Since in the late 60's and early 70's I was usually the only WECT reporter in the field, as Ken had been made News Director and anchor, I was expected to bring back at least four or five complete stories every afternoon, then sit down and write them into final form in time for the newscast.

Old Reliable…simple to use and almost indestrutructible

I found out that if I started my day with breakfast at the Dixie Café, the morning gathering place of lawyers, politicians, judges and business leaders, I usually left with enough leads to keep me busy all day.

Today, with the big news staffs and crews of dozens, I wonder how Ken and I managed to fill up our allotted half hour with real news, not features and fluff, and still keep our sanity.

In fact, we fought for every available second of news time, sometimes resorting to borrowing a few minutes from weather or sports if there was something especially important to report.

News was a whole different animal back then. That was before the day of Happy-chatty chitchat between anchors, reporters, meteorologists, etc. We didn't think of news as entertainment…it was, well, NEWS, and every air minute was precious and important to fill with NEWS.

Speaking now from my vantage point of 74 years, I sometimes cringe at what I hear on the air. Then, there was an unspoken rule among reporters that we didn't pry into private lives unless their conduct somehow interfered with a public trust or was an integral part of the breaking news story. Our word of confidentiality to a source was taken seriously, and we were expected to absolutely, positively confirm our stories before they were aired.

Recently, I could hardly believe my ears when a respected Network Anchor began a story with the phrase "It is rumored that…" An opening like that would have brought Wayne Jackson bearing a pink slip to your office in no time flat.

I realize that today TV reporters and anchors have to deal with an onslaught of competition for the all-news cable channels as well as more local sources, and that places on them what must be an unending conflict between getting it on first and getting it on right.

There also seems to be a changing expectation from the viewing audience who appear to want their news to be both informative and at the same time entertaining…two elements that don't necessarily combine well.

Perhaps the more informal way of presenting the news, and the on-camera involvement of reporters as a part of the event that is happening forms a closer and more personal connection between reporter and viewer. I don't know.

I don't mind admitting that I'm old enough to be part of that time in journalism when you were taught that a reporter reported…not participated. Our guideline, I suppose, was "What would Walter Cronkite do?"

My almost ten years as a TV news reporter left me with many memories, some funny, some sad, some frightening. I had to learn to look at murder and accident victims with a certain detachment. I learned how to keep out of the way of firemen and policemen and still get the story. I learned that even a reporter cries at the funeral of a police officer killed in the line of duty.

The immediacy of television also presented a dilemma more pressing than that of print journalism…the sometimes very brief period between covering a story and getting it on the air. It had better be right the first time, because that first time was what listeners remembered, whether or not you changed, explained, or apologized for a mistake later.

I don't think this has really changed, but apparently in the all-consuming competitive race for ratings and "exclusives", it has become more accepted when the first version of the story turns out to be, well, not quite as reported.

Along the way, sound-on-film came along, allowing me to do on the spot interviews and stories. I remember learning during that time not to ask stupid questions.

Following the bombing of the building which housed the black newspaper "The Wilmington Journal" on its lower floor, I interviewed the occupant of an upstairs apartment who was literally blown out of bed by the explosion.

After a few preliminary questions I inanely asked "Did it scare you?"

"Lady", the shaken man answered, "It scared the s— out of me!" Some quick editing was in order when that film got back to the studio.

I also remember the eerie feeling of suddenly realizing a truth as I stood on the bank of a creek in Brunswick County. I watched the body of a young murder victim bob up and down in the water as law enforcement officers and reporters waited for the coroner to arrive.

Among the bystanders was the youth who had stumbled into the Sheriff's Department early that morning, telling them that he and the young man who now floated in the creek were victims of a robbery-kidnapping the night before. He, he said, had managed to escape.

As I talked to the teenager and his father, I began to realize that something didn't make sense. His answers were too pat, too detailed. Something wasn't right! I casually wandered over to my photographer and told him to take pictures…lots of pictures…of that young man.

"He did it," I said, "or he knows exactly who did." It turned out later in court that the whole robbery-kidnapping had been a faked set-up by the two teenagers and an older man to cover up the very real robbery of the two service stations where the two younger men worked.

When one of the two teenagers wanted to back out of the conspiracy the fake kidnapping turned into the real thing, ending in his murder. The image of that young boy floating face down in the muddy waters of the creek while his assailant casually looked down at him is something that will forever stay in my memory.

Another vivid memory is of the night that I was assigned, all by myself, to cover a full-dress "formal" cross-burning by the KKK. I drove up to the isolated field where a huge cross was flaming, and parked my little yellow station wagon. Hooded figures moved in shadowy circles around the burning cross.

As I got out of the car a jack-booted, militarily garbed figure loomed up in front of me and demanded, "What do you want?"

Startled, the first thing that popped out of my mouth was "Take me to your leader."

He did. I was ushered into to purple- silk- robed presence of the Grand Dragon himself and, not to miss an opportunity, I started to interview him. After a few questions the Grand Dragon paused, cocked his head and inquired "Betty?"

Turns out that the awesome Grand Dragon was a rather non-descript, barely noticeable kid that I had gone to high school with. So much for the "awesome" part!

I suppose that the most stressful, most demanding story that I ever covered was the ten-day period of racial rioting in February of 1971. That was really a learning experience. I dodged gunfire and saw people shot. I watched innocent people terrified and people who should have known better incite more violence.

I found out how hard it can be to remain objective when your mind is reeling from something you have just encountered, or when someone you know and respect does something incredibly stupid, underhanded, or even illegal and you have a responsibility to report on it.

I encountered for the first time the arrogance of some members of the "big-city" press, some of whom arrived in Wilmington with their stories already written full-blown in their heads and who didn't want to be bothered with hearing any facts. Sometimes, reading their wire-service stories the next day I wondered if we had really even been at the same places at the same time…but I remembered seeing them there!

I also watched Wayne, and Ken and Dan Cameron agonize over what and how to cover the events…what would make things worse and what might help make things better.

That, I think, is a large part of what television news should be…a sense of responsibility to the people you're talking to, and to the people you're talking about.

I realize that with the proliferation of cable news, the outpouring of Internet information, the all-consuming race for the ratings, and the pressure to be politically correct it is easy for TV news to be carried along with the prevailing attitudes. But I still believe that the paragraph above is what it is all about!

Day or Night, WECT News was there !!

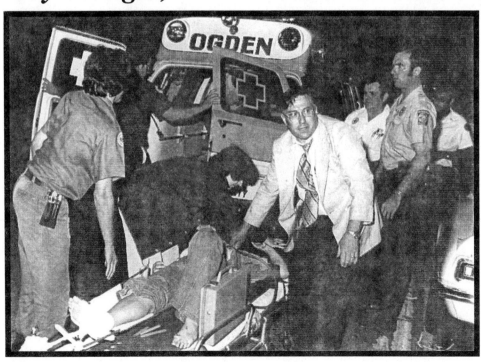

When Things Happened,

Our News team was on the scene of train wrecks..

...and plane crashes

138

Wect News Was There . . .

Lumina Pavilon at Wrightsville Beach, the scene of balls and Big Band performances, fell to disrepair and the wrecker's ball.

Federal agents recover radioactive materials stolen from the GE Nuclear facility

When Things Happened,

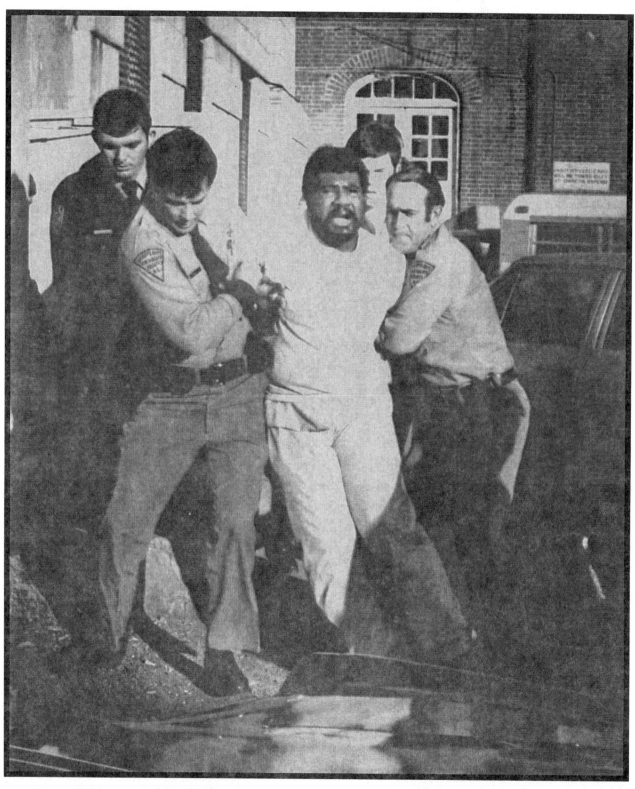

Allan Hall, one of the Wilmington 10, struggles with Sheriff's deputies after his conviction on riot-related charges.

Wect News Was There . . .

*Activist Angela Davis and the Soledad Brothers came to Wilmington
during the period of racial upheaval in 1971-72*

The National Guard was brought in to help control rioting in 1968 and '71

When Things Happened,

Above: the Coast Guard tows the captured drug-laden vessel Sea Crust into dock in downtown Wilmington.

Left: DEA Agents load tons of baled marijuana into a truck after removing it from the hold of the seized ship. The drugs had a street value in excess of a million dollars.

Wect News Was There . . .

Above: Smoke billows from the fire at the Sutton Coucil furniture store on Front Street. The area is now the site of the historic Cotton Exchange shopping complex. The Fire Department was able to minimize damage to many of the more than 100 year old buildings.

Right: WECT Chief Photographer C.L. Perkins climbs the aerial ladder to get a better shot of the Sutton Council fire

When Things Happened,

WECT photographer C.L. Perkins films an interview with Wilmington native and NBC News Anchor Davis Brinkley in front of the Bellamy mansion. The man at left is an NBC producer...the segment was for use on the Today Show.

Wect News Was There...

Ronald Reagan and his wife Nancy (right) brought his presidential campaign to the streets of Wilmington, meeting and greeting local residents.

Snowfall at the beach in 1973 was an event..so we covered it

Wect News Was There...

In 1973, the proposed consolidation of the city and county was a hotly debated issue. In 2004...it still is.

Still Here...and No Regrets

Ken Murphy
News Anchor, News Director, Commentator
1965 until present

Ken Murphy waits in the rain for the start of televised ceremonies opening the Cape Fear Memorial Bridge

I heard about an opening at WECT from George Deaton, with whom I had worked at WIDU radio in Fayetteville after I mustered out of the Air Force (George had already migrated to Wilmington.). It's a good thing, too, because I learned that the radio station was going to change its format from "pop" to "ethnic," and I wasn't ethnic enough to continue working there.

I drove my 1964 ½ white Mustang convertible to Wilmington, with the top down, and interviewed with Wayne Jackson, who was Program Manager of WECT (In those days, you also had to do an "audition," by reading some wire copy on camera.).

I passed.

I came to work at WECT fully expecting to be there no longer than a year - contracts were unknown at the time - live at the beach, get that long-held desire out of my system, and then go on with my career. Having worked at WBTV in Charlotte one summer (I was a Jefferson Standard, now Jefferson Pilot, scholar) I had already tasted The Big Time, and intended to get back into that environment. But I had underestimated the charm of the Wilmington environment and the satisfaction that comes from working with people who became my family-away-from-home.

So, nearly forty years later, here I am, not rich and famous (just infamous), but with no regrets.

Some of the highlights of those nearly four decades at WECT include: the Cameron and Brody brothers buying out Roy Park (who was notoriously tight-fisted-our original building had cinderblock interior walls and no carpeting) who also owned a controlling interest in WNCT in Greenville. We wanted to erect a new 2,000-foot tower near White Lake so that nearly half our broadcast signal would not be squandered over the ocean. But the signal would overlap WNCT's, and the FCC said that was a duopoly and we couldn't do it. Eventually, the deal was done, the move was made, and our A-grade broadcast signal stretched from Wilmington to Fayetteville, instead of from Elizabethtown to forty miles offshore. In the interim, our building has been added onto four or five times, much of it tastefully decorated.

Certainly, some of the news highlights I've seen included: building the Memorial Bridge over the river. Granted, it was only mid-level and still required traffic interruptions, but it was a great improvement over the old '20s-era bridges over the Northeast and Cape Fear Rivers, which was the only way in and out of town. All traffic no longer had to wend its way through downtown, and congestion was greatly relieved. Many an afternoon was spent lolling on the riverbank near the foot of Castle Street watching and filming the progress.

Another was an "Unpleasantness," but it signaled an evolution in race relations in the city. That was the civil strife that erupted following the assassination of Dr. Martin Luther King, Jr., in 1968, and the desegregation of the schools in the early '70's. They were difficult times, but the city emerged changed for the better.

All the while, WECT was evolving too. We became a full-color station, i.e., we put color cameras in the studio, and began using color film instead of black-and-white. Soon, film itself went the way of the dodo with the introduction of videotape cameras and editing equipment. Previously, after the film was processed, it had to be physically cut and spliced together with glue.

Electronic journalism equipment, as it was called, was much easier and versatile. No processing was required, and edits were made with "in points" and "out points" instead of razor blades and cement. At first, even that was so prodigiously bulky that we actually had to use a hand truck to move the equipment around. Nowadays, stuff that accomplishes the same thing can easily be held in just one hand (but I recommend using a tripod).

Then, along came digital video-video with such high resolution, it was better than film. We already shoot and edit news tapes in a digital format, and the station is in the process of installing digital broadcast equipment, in addition to our familiar "analog" equipment that produces your current picture. If you can afford the set, you can get a wide-screen (wider than Cinemascope movies even) picture at home with such high definition and marvelous audio you'll swear you are looking at the real thing.

So, since I've been at WECT, we've gone from grainy, black-and-white pictures that suffered frequent interference and with tinny monaural sound, to something approaching a real viewing experience. Wonder what's next?

Ken Murphy's Commentary

I was not, as some have suggested, a witness to the invention of television. Philo T. Farnsworth (I didn't make that name up!) got the idea in 1920. He was outstanding in his field. Literally, he was plowing, and noticing the rows of furrows, had a flash of insight that maybe he could use that new invention called radio to send bits of information in rows like that. We would later call them scanning lines. It was six years later before Farnsworth managed to send a rudimentary picture through the air to a receiver. But, the threshold was crossed. David Sarnoff, head of the communications giant RCA, tried unsuccessfully for years to claim the patent. He lost, but he didn't lose any money, using his pull to push Farnsworth out of the race.

Enough history. Suffice it to say, commercial television was able in just a quarter-century to turn itself into a "vast wasteland," as FCC Chairman Newton Minnow once described it. I think someone had just rained on Minnow's parade that day. True, television wastes a lot of time, but nowadays it has a lot of time to waste. It's a far cry from the days when you were lucky to get three stations, one for each network, even with an outside antenna. Cable was available only in a limited area, and it largely just rebroadcast the air signals it could pull in with its very large antennas. Selection was meager, complaints were often ignored. But things have changed.

With cable offering literally hundreds of channels, filling every preferred niche and some no one ever heard of, TV is vast, but not a wasteland.

Which also means that local stations, like the one I work for, compete directly with those multi-channel outlets, and they do that largely with local news and local programming. That's something you can't get on the "upper tier," like the History Channel and the Discovery Channel, and A&E, and the Learning Channel, which though fine as they are, don't tell you what's going on at City Hall, who robbed a bank this afternoon, and other items of local curiosity.

Frankly, I think television is great. I just can't wait 'til I can afford one of those wide-screen plasma deals with neighbor-irritating sound capabilities.

By 1974 both studio facilities and equipment had become more sophisticated. On the News, Weather and Sports sets are (l to r) Les Paternotte, Kleist Wideman, Ken Murphy, Jim Burns, Tom Sweeney, and Bob Townsend

Production Manager Ernie Whitmire (foreground) checks a taped commercial. The advent of video tape added greatly to WECT's capabilities.

In Retrospect

Dan Cameron

"I'd have to say I had a very enjoyable 35 years in the television business. Like any other business, you had ups and downs but I can't think of many times that it was not enjoyable. It was always upbeat, you dealt with upbeat people. The staff had a certain temperament that was almost always positive and it was a fun business."

In the thirties Mr. Richard Dunlea was a radio operator stationed on a Coast Guard boat here. His ambition was to start a commercial radio station in Wilmington. I don't know the exact circumstances, but my father met Mr. Dunlea and helped finance the new enterprise and became a partner for 40% of the ownership. Thus was radio station WMFD built and put on the air.

The enterprise was a success so when the F.C.C. approved an allocation for a TV station in this area Mr. Dunlea, along with the MacMillan and Cameron Company, which my family owned, agreed to participate with the same percentage interest that we held in the radio station.

The F.C.C. granted the license to us, as we were the only applicant. The television station, WMFD-TV, went on the air in 1954. Mr. Dunlea and his son, Richard Jr., who was just out of college, did a great job of hiring the original staff (mostly from radio) and getting the station on the air.

Dan Cameron

As there were not many television sets in use during the early 50's, it was hard to sell advertising to the local businesses and the station showed a substantial loss for the first several years. Our prospects didn't look good.

After a few years the Dunleas came to us with a buy or sell proposition; we could name the price and they would have thirty days to decide if they wanted to buy or sell. We set a price and I remember saying to my brother Bruce that our TV days were over.

To our surprise they elected to sell. Instead of buying their interest entirely ourselves we contacted the Brody family in Kinston, owners of the Wilmington radio station WGNI and also the owners of the Greenville TV station. We convinced them that they would be better off to buy into our station than to pursue the idea of opening another TV station, which had recently been allocated to Wilmington.

Both parties bought the idea so we ended up with a four-way ownership that included the Cameron family for 30%, the Brody family for 30%, the Greenville TV station for 30%, and Mr. J.W. Jackson for 10%.

At that time we reorganized and I was asked to serve as President on a temporary basis until we could install a permanent manager who had television experience.

My service in the capacity of president was to last for a happy 30 years.

Of course there were challenges. In the very early days the biggest challenge was… we didn't have any business! We had a staff to pay and had to stay on the air, but we didn't have any advertisers.

The problem was that the merchants were used to buying a one-minute radio spot for a dollar and our price was $25, which they thought was outrageous. At first the Dunleas had a policy that if somebody wouldn't pay $25 for a spot, they wouldn't sell it. But we immediately changed that policy since we figured if we lost a minute of advertising, we would never be able to get it back.

We developed a package deal. I remember going down to Mr. Fred Willetts, who ran the Cooperative Savings & Loan. He was a big advertiser but he wouldn't buy television because he said it cost too much, so I went down and laid out a proposal for him, offering him $40,000 worth of television time in one year. He hit the ceiling and said he wasn't about to spend that much money. I said, "Wait a minute, you haven't heard the rest of my deal… I'm going to sell it to you for $15,000 if you will pay in advance."

He agreed to that and that same day I went to the Carolina Savings and Loan, their greatest rivals, and presented the same deal to Mr. Fonville and he bought it and so, I went to Mr. Jackson at the Pepsi Cola plant, offered him the same deal and he bought it… and all three of them agreed to pay in advance.

Then I went to Mr. John Fox at Fox's Bakery and he said " I'll take the deal, but I can't pay you in advance".

I said, " That's all right, let's make a deal". So in that one day we sold $60,000 worth of television time and got $40,000 in the bank… which we desperately needed. I had learned that sales policies, and prices, had to be flexible when you're selling a new media.

One of the things that really helped our sales was that by then people were buying television sets like crazy. The sets were all black and white; we only had one network affiliation, NBC, but we were the only TV station in town. There were huge numbers of television sets during that time, and if you didn't have a set you just weren't with it. You would see little antennas in the most unlikely places. It might be a little junky house, but it would have a TV antenna on it.

I remember when we got our first television set at home, which was pretty early on since our family business, MacMillan and Cameron, sold TV sets. We sold thousands of sets as soon as WMFD-TV went on the air. They were pretty expensive at first but our store, like most other businesses then, had a time payment system. We would sell a set for a dollar down and a dollar when we could catch you. We sold hundreds of them because everybody wanted one. They weren't hard to sell. Everybody had to have one.

And because we were the only station in the area, we could "cherry pick" ABC and CBS, which meant that if they had a program that was really popular we could make a deal to carry it and substitute it for one that would normally be on NBC. After all, we were the only station in this area. In that way, we could offer the most popular shows from all three networks.

The Brodys, originally from Kinston, were a big family, very successful. They had stores in Kinston and some in South Carolina and Greenville, North Carolina. The medical center in Greenville has recently been named the Brody School of Medicine because different members of the family have given over $20 million to the medical school there.

The main task I had was getting good people to do all the various jobs, and in this I was very fortunate. We ended up with a terrific staff who knew what they were doing. I got a general manager in to help me because when we branched off into the television enterprise I had to spend a lot of time developing that, but we always had good people at the station.

Claud O'Shields was the general manager. He worked at the station for many years and he also became a county commissioner. Then his son, Buck O'Shields, came to work for us when he was about 20 years old. He too ended up being a county commissioner. Then I had C.D. Martin, who was the sales manager. He was the perfect sales manager; everybody liked him and he really knew how to sell.

***Standing: C.D. Martin, Sales Manager;
Claud O'Shields, Gen. Manager;
seated: Clint Long, Program Director;
and R.A. Dunlea Jr., President, WMFD-TV***

Since television was a new industry, we got a lot of our talent from radio. In fact, at first almost everybody was from radio, and the way they learned to make the switch from one media to the other was really amazing. It was interesting to see how they could take a programming or production idea that had worked well on radio and adapt it to work well on television.

Wayne Jackson came to work for us really early on, also from radio, and he was the program manager and a very savvy guy. He had the early morning program for years. He was just a good man to have around. And he had a great voice, which was very important.

We had a little party several years ago and we invited all the people who had been at the television station from the years 1954 to 1974. We expected maybe to get 40 or 50 people and ended up with 130 people. They came in from New York and the west coast and Florida and Atlanta. We had a grand time. It was a fabulous reunion. A lot of them have done really well in television and in other businesses too.

Very early on WMFD-TV decided we needed a local news show. We had a character that people around Wilmington still remember, Ben McDonald. When I took the station over, he would go on the air with a walk like Walter Winchell and he talked like Walter Winchell. We finally made him take his trade-mark fedora off when he was on the air, but he was unconventional, to say the least, and he was our 6:00 newsman for a while, for a good long while.

Local news coverage was very important because...until then, there was no local news on television.

We went on the air at 6:00 in the morning and had our own morning show to give that important local flavor. We also had a noontime show with Jim Burns, who worked for us for 28 years. He had a daytime show and he was a kind of a catch-up person. Anybody who had something they wanted to talk about would want to get on Jim's show. He interviewed everybody from Book Club members to wild animal handlers.

I wish we had some of those early shows on tape but of course, we didn't have tape machines then. We had one camera...a really big bulky affair. Having just one camera we had to swing it back and forth between live shots and, say, commercials... back and forth. It was really a mess at times, and took real coordination.

You must realize that when we first went on, our antenna was just across the river and we had a very, very narrow coverage area. It covered Wilmington and that was about it. A lot of signal went out into the ocean...and fish don't buy advertising...and so the first thing Mr. Dunlea did was to move from the little radio antenna he was using right across the river and put a 1000 foot antenna up at Delco. That expanded our coverage considerably, but we still weren't getting out very far; we got to Whiteville then and the fringes of Myrtle Beach. That was about it, just Southeastern North Carolina.

Later, in the early 60s, one of the most important moves that we made was to relocate our antenna to White Lake up near Elizabethtown and built the tallest man-made structure east of the Mississippi River. We put that tower 2000 feet up in the air and that gave us Fayetteville, Lumberton, edges of Jacksonville and Myrtle Beach. It increased our coverage tremendously. NBC did not have any TV coverage at all in any of those areas so that was a smart move on our part.

Then of course we had to expand our local coverage to include all those areas. That was one of the things Wayne Jackson did so well; he would go to all these little communities and we'd do interviews and televise things that were going on, letting them know that we were interested in them too. We tried to encompass all of those communities.

Of course, being able to "cherry pick" programs from networks other that NBC didn't last forever. When Channel 3 went on the air in 1963 they took all the ABC programs. We were still able to take some CBS programming but I don't think the station does any CBS now because they have their own coverage and cable and everything.

While it lasted, thought, "cherry picking" was a powerful tool. For example we carried " I Love Lucy" which was a CBS program, Andy Griffith was very popular, and we were able to carry that too. And of course all the networks competed to convince us to carry their shows.

Since it was the first opportunity that people in Wilmington had to actually meet the people they saw on TV, almost every staff member and local person who appeared on the air became sort of instant celebrities.

One who became very popular and stayed that way for years was Jim Burns. He was popular because he was accessible and he got all kinds of groups, the ladies society, the   missionary groups, anybody who had some special item to sell or cause to promote wanted to appear on his show. He had an hour-long program and people loved to be on the Jim Burns show. He was a very good emcee, not a comic, but he had a good sense of humor. He would go out to community meetings and ribbon cuttings and he talked to people all day long on the telephone. He was an effective ambassador of good will.

The other media in town took different views of us; the newspaper saw us as competition and tried to ignore us, while the radio stations, they just kept on doing what they were doing, and they've done well. I don't know how many radio stations we have in town now, but it's a lot.

As time passed, the technology of television evolved and changed and we had to keep up with it. We went from a basic operation with one camera, later to tape machines, which was quite a leap. The tape then wasn't like video tape, though…it went through the studio camera.

Those tape machines were as big as the wall in the control room and the camera fed those machines. Great big reels, and of course that was a great revolution. Before that, we could show film, we could show an old movie with a movie sort of setup, but tape made a big, big, difference.

Old movies were a story in themselves. We had to pay to use them, of course, and lots of stuff was available, old black and white films. Some of them were pretty bad but you could kill an hour's air time with an old movie.

And of course we carried NBC's national news featuring a hometown boy named David Brinkley, who was a big hit here in Wilmington. He was an anchor on the Huntley-Brinkley Report and they were a powerful team for a long time.

NBC later let him go and he went to ABC and was a star over there. We always thought NBC was dumb to let David Brinkley get away.

As the fifties drew to a close we realized that we were quickly outgrowing our facilities in downtown Wilmington. The inconvenient third floor studio with its two flights of stairs and squeaky floors was just not adequate anymore, so we began planning a new building to be designed especially for television. That studio, located on Shipyard Boulevard, is still used by WECT-TV although it has been enlarged a number of times since then.

Then, in the early sixties, color television made its debut. And that stuff cost so much money. It was difficult when you weren't making much money and you had to go out and buy this expensive equipment, but color made a big difference and of course we went from one studio camera to two cameras…a giant step for a small station. In those days a camera cost tens of thousands of dollars, so it wasn't a step we took lightly.

As to portability, we had cameras that we could go out and take pictures with but at that time we didn't have tape machines. We'd have to go out, do the film, come back in, develop the film, run it through and put it on the air. Sometimes film of late-breaking stories was still being edited as the news show began.

Our local news time ran from 6 to 6:30pm, and it was a labor-intensive product. The news department was always the most expensive part of the operation because you had to get talented people and had to get good reporters and it took a lot of coordination to take all the rough material and zero it down to a half hour. We always tried to keep enough people out working to bring the news in. For a little station it was a burden but it was necessary because we were selling local news, something they couldn't provide on the network.

Once in a while a story from Wilmington even made the national news, but it was usually a hurricane or something like that…something we didn't need!

Then later there came another big change, cable. I was in the group, my brother and I, that brought cable to Wilmington originally. It was going to come so we joined in the group for the franchise and we put the original cable in Wilmington. I figured somebody was going to do it; we might as well be part of it.

We hadn't been in it too long and had just gotten to where we were making money when somebody a lot smarter than we were bought us out. It's now Time-Warner.

In those days, you could own seven television stations; you could have five VHF stations and two UHF stations. We had only one television station; the FCC said you could own seven, and I can tell you a story about that.

After we had had the station for a while, we started making money and my stockholders wanted, instead of taking dividends out of the station, to buy something else so they commissioned me to look around and find another broadcasting property. I presented several things to the board and Mr. J. W. Jackson, who was the Pepsi Cola man on our board and was about 70 years old, said "Why don't you boys buy my Pepsi business?"

We hadn't even thought of that and had no idea he wanted to sell the Pepsi business. He said he had reached a stage in life where he'd like to unload and he would like to sell it to us.

To make a long story short, we bought the Wilmington Pepsi Cola plant from Mr. Jackson and that put us in the Pepsi business. In other words, the television station bought the Pepsi business as an investment.

So we ran the Pepsi business here. Then just by chance an opportunity came along to buy four Pepsi operations in Columbia, South Carolina. We didn't have the money to do it, so we sold the local Pepsi operation, made a little money on that, and using that as a down payment, bought the four plants down in Columbia and Rock Hill, Sumter and Orangeburg and then we then had four Pepsi Cola operations. The expanding that we did over the years after that was in the Pepsi Cola franchise and not in television.

We ended up buying 14 Pepsi Cola bottling operations and stayed in it for about 20 years, until the Corporation sold it in 1979.

And all through that time period, late 50s, 60s, 70s and 80s, the economy wasn't always up, and when it was down, we were well aware of it in the television business. But even when the economy wasn't too good, we ran pretty steadily. We had a super sales force and when things got bad, we'd try to convince the merchants that advertising would improve their lot so we always, I think, had a pretty good product to sell.

But people just don't walk in to buy your ads…you have to have a super sales force. We had a fellow here in town; he's still here, Joe Schlegal, who was just a super salesman. He could get blood out of a turnip, as the saying goes. He was very popular.

And what we were really selling was exposure for their product or service, and that exposure kept growing as more and more households had television sets. I think in the 60s just about every household had a television set.

After all, advertising was, and still is the main source of money for a TV station. That's local advertising. People may think that a lot of money comes from the network advertising but that is actually a very small part of the overall income.

We would produce our own commercials, and the production was a part of our whole package. If you bought an ad and you wanted to sell an automobile, we would work through it with you to show that car and where you could get it. Usually our copywriters wrote the commercials; sometimes the advertisers wanted to do it themselves. In fact, some of them wanted their own people to be in the commercials. Sometimes they got very creative, and some of them loved to star their whole families in the ads, but we were pretty flexible about that.

Today there are a lot of production companies here in Wilmington that a merchant or advertiser can hire to produce their commercials entirely…then the station simply has to run it. But for a long time we were the only production people.

I've always considered our news people a very important aspect of our business. They have to be personable and they have to have credibility. Every news story is, or should be, important to some viewer and should be presented that way. I think we've been fortunate to have some fine people, both reporters and anchors, over the years.

I hired Ken Murphy and I hired Frances Weller. Kenneth has been with the station nearly 40 years now, and he's been the anchorman for all those years. Frances has been there darn near 20 years and those two have carried the burden of the local news. We have a lot of youngsters that come in to learn the trade and then move to their own places. But Frances and Ken have both stuck with us.

Now let me tell you about the evolution of the weather person, because now that seems to be one of the most important people that a station has. This is a fairly new development. We had weather, we had a weatherman, but any of our on-the-air people could do weather. They just needed a pleasant personality, a good voice, and be able to think on their feet.

We didn't have degreed meteorologists and we didn't have the Dopplers. We never had a meteorologist but we still got the weather out pretty good. I get a kick out of watching Channel 3 and Channel 6 fight about who's got the greatest radar.

As far as the day-to-day operation of the station, I always considered myself a delegator, absolutely. My hands were in so many pies I didn't have time to handle details. I'm not a good detail man anyhow. I'm an idea person. Some station executives like to participate in every detail of the operation but I just have a different style.

I thoroughly enjoyed the thirty years I spent in television, but in 1987 we came to the decision that it was time to move on. Our business partners were both getting old, one of then was ill, and it just seemed like it was a good time to liquidate.

We had people in those days eager to buy T.V. stations so it was not a hard thing to sell at a good price. The group as a whole just decided that this was a good time to get out of the business. I was over 65 years old and you know when you get to be 65, you start to think a little bit about what's left. It just seemed like a good thing to do.

We made arrangements with a very well known media broker and he brought us our customer. We sold to a newspaper from St. Louis, Missouri who also had television stations at that time. The station has been bought and sold three times since then.

I'd have to say I had a very enjoyable 30 years in the television business. Like any other business, you had ups and downs. I can't think of many times that it was not enjoyable. It was always upbeat; you dealt with upbeat people. The staff had a certain temperament that was always, not always, but almost always positive... and it was a fun business. I found the television business fascinating back then, and I still do.

NOTE: The preceding was compiled from interviews with Dan Cameron conducted for the UNCW Randall University Library by University Librarian Sherman Hayes, UNCW Archivist Adina Riggins, and Paul Zarbuck, Special Consultant to the University Librarian.

The GOOD Times

Frequent staff parties and get-togethers were a part of the close-knit atmosphere of those first 20 years. Here, Dan Cameron does the cooking at a mullet roast.

CHANNEL 6
1954-1974

TWENTY YEARS OF SERVICE

WECT-TV

MILESTONES TO REMEMBER
WMFD-TV - WECT-TV

Friday, April 9ᵗʰ, 1954...The First Day on the Air
Sign on 7:00 PM - Sign off 11:59:30 PM

Monday, Sept. 7, 1954... First Daytime Programming
4:30-5:55   Relax with Jax

Friday, Feb. 18, 1955...First Live Network

3:00	Greatest Gift, NBC	3:15.. Relax with Jax
3:30	One Man's Family, NBC	3:45.. Relax with Jax
4:00	Hawkin's Falls, NBC	4:30.. Relax with Jax
5:00	Pinkie Lee, NBC	4:45..Kiddie Time
5:30	Howdy Doody, NBC	
8:30	Life of Riley, NBC	
10:00	Gillette Cavalcade of Sports, NBC	

Monday, Oct. 1, 1956...First CBS and Morning Programs

11:15	Love of Life, CBS
11:45	Guiding Light, CBS
1:30	Tennessee Ernie Ford, NBC
2:00	Matinee Theater, NBC
3:00	Brighter Day, CBS
3:15	Secret Storm, CBS
3:30	Edge of Night, CBS

**Saturday, June 1, 1957...New 1000 Tower, Full Power
at Delco Transmitter Site**

9:00 AM	Howdy Doody, NBC
At night	Perry Como, George Gobel, Hit Parade

Monday, June 3, 1957...All Day Programming Begins

7:00 AM	Today, NBC
9:00	Home, NBC
10:00	Price is Right, NBC
10:30	Strike It Rich, CBS
11:15	Love of Life, CBS
11:30	Local News, Studio
11:45	Guiding Light, CBS
1:00	Cooking Can Be Fun, Studio